Fast and Flawless

A guide to airless spraying

Pete Wilkinson
www.fastandflawless.co.uk

First published in the United Kingdom in 2016

Copyright © Pete Wilkinson

Pete Wilkinson has asserted his right to be identified as the author of this work in accordance with the Copyright, Designs and Patents Act 1988

All rights reserved. No part of this publication may be reproduced, stored in a retrieval system, or transmitted in any form or by any means, electronic, mechanical, photocopying, recording or otherwise, without prior permission of the copyright owner.

This book is not intended to provide personalised legal, financial, or investment advice. The Author and Publisher specifically disclaim any liability, loss or risk which is incurred as a consequence, directly or indirectly of the use and application of any contents of this.

Updated for 2020

21-07-2020

6 X 9

Thanks to Stephen Smith Decorators for giving me the opportunity to spray student apartments.

Thanks to Fine Finish Decorators aka Mark Watts for proof reading the first draft.

Thanks to Dennis Kehoe Ltd for giving me an apprenticeship which has changed my life for the better.

Thanks to Tracey for inspiring me to follow my dreams.

What people are saying about Fast and Flawless

For those of you who have bought the print version of the book, here are some of the reviews taken from Amazon.

I found this book by accident. I was a decorator looking to get in to the spraying side after watching the Idaho painter on YouTube, he made it look easy, so I thought I could give it a go. I bought a machine and off I went. Well everything went wrong you could think of, couldn't get the paint to come out of the gun! So I searched online and this book came up. I can honestly say this book is like the bible for the serious decorator who wants to spray. It gives you straight forward information, in an easy to read format. Once I had read the book I knew exactly where I was going wrong. Anyway after a few spray jobs (spending ages masking up) I thought I better go on a course, so I booked on a recommended course and who was the teacher? Mr fast and flawless himself! Pete is a genuine guy who wants to help others step their game up and provide that flawless finish for customers. Even if you are not a decorator, this book will help you get going with spraying. Spraying is the future! – Bradboy

Whether you're a seasoned sprayer or complete novice, this book is a great reference for when you're spraying something different. When you know what tip to use but not sure what pressure, when that spray pattern just doesn't look right or you're using a different paint. Written by a sprayer, for sprayers. – Mark E

As a novice sprayer starting out it was recommended to me to buy this book. It wasn't filled with loads of jargon but clear precise instructions, hints and tips that were easy to understand. Read it in a couple of nights and I've re-read it a couple of times since, a good addition to anyone's spray kit for reference. – Clayton

Great book really enjoyed the read. Thank you to the author for the time taken to write this book. A must read for any serious decorator – Jonny

The only reference tool anyone could ever need irrespective of their experience levels in Airless spraying. Pete's comprehensive knowledge, experience and passion for the subject shines through from start to finish. It's like one of those novels that you never want to put down as there is always something more interesting and informative on the next page! Also, it's written in an engaging laid back chatty style which is an absolute joy to read, but also all the technical stuff is in there too, and so easy to understand, which is a huge bonus. Pete is a natural teacher and is also one of life's genuine nice guys too. Buy the book, trust me you will never regret it! – Stephen

These are just a few comments that I have picked out, this is the reason I originally wrote the book, to help and guide decorators down the road of airless spraying. These comments have made it all worthwhile. If you enjoy the book, then please leave a review for me on Amazon.

Contents

Preface – Page 9

A little bit of background about the book.

Chapter 1 – Introduction – Page 13

This is about the book and why I wrote it.

Chapter 2 – Training – Page 32

An insight into the world of training.

Chapter 3 – Types of sprayers – Page 46

Looking at how systems differ, Conventional, HVLP, XVLP and airless.

Chapter 4 – Companies and what they offer – Page 60

There are a lot of different companies and sprayers out there. This chapter gives a flavour of what is available.

Chapter 5 – Essential equipment – Page 87

The pump, the hose, the gun, tools. This chapter discusses what makes up an airless system and which tools to use.

Chapter 6 – Using the equipment – Page 113

How do you go about spraying? This chapter looks at setting up the system and actually spraying.

Chapter 7 – Masking – Page 141

It's surprising how many people do not know the basics of masking. Here we explore how to mask common items.

Chapter 8 – PPE – Page 167

The all-important health and safety chapter.

Chapter 9 – A bit about paint – Page 174

A bit of paint technology for all you apprentice and student readers.

Chapter 10 – When it all goes wrong – Page 188

Some common problems you may encounter when spraying and how to remedy them.

Chapter 11 – Spraying in the real world – Page 198

Here we discuss the common myths and objections to spraying.

Chapter 12 – Pricing for profit – Page 208

If you decide to start spraying, then you need to get your pricing right.

Chapter 13 – Common paint defects – Page 219

Looking at the common ways that paint can fail and the way to fix it.

Chapter 14 - The last one – Page 233

A few parting words.

Preface

Four years ago, I was sat in my lounge chatting with Tracey about what I wanted to do with my new found freedom. I had gone part time from college and I now had two whole days where I could do whatever I wanted. I had started doing some decorating work and I was specialising in spraying. I had taught both HVLP and airless spraying at college for many years and I was enjoying getting back on the tools and actually spraying for real.

My passion has always been to make a difference to the decorating industry and to some extent I have been doing this at college, however I had limited influence because the apprentices that I taught were at the start of their career and in most cases were more interested in what they would be doing Friday night with their mates than learning about decorating. In fairness some of my students have gone on to build their own businesses and this is very rewarding for me, however it's a very long game.

I wanted to train experienced decorators who were working in the industry. My main focus was to teach them how to use airless sprayers to improve their productivity. I had quite a few enquiries for me to go on site and do some training. I was keen to do this, and I felt I would be good at it. One of the things I wanted to do at the end of the day spent training with them was to give the decorator a reference book on airless spraying.

I searched on Amazon (like you do) and found……..

Nothing.

I was amazed. "There is no book on airless spraying available" I told my wife Tracey. "Isn't that amazing?"

"I am going to write one" I said.

At that moment a little voice in my head said, "That's never going to happen Pete."

However, I started to write. Every Monday night I got out my laptop and typed. I found the words flowed out. This was actually quite enjoyable. The book started to take shape and before I knew it (6 months later) I had something that I could send to print.

Not finished, full of spelling mistakes but something I could print. I sent the file off to the printers and waited for the proof to arrive. The day it arrived was so exciting, I know it sounds a bit sad, but it was. A real book! That I had written. Wow.

I posted a picture of this proof copy on Twitter. Immediately I was inundated with requests to buy the book! Happy days. Only one problem. It was not really finished or properly edited. I spent the next week finishing the book and editing it.

Time has gone by and I have sold quite a few copies to decorators around the world. I have had some really good feedback from decorators, and it has been a rewarding experience.

The onsite training developed, and I decided it would be great to deliver training in a workshop so that I could cover all aspects of spraying, not just what the job needed. I was lucky, in that I had a good friend who had a workshop he was not using. It was an empty space full of empty paint tins and dustsheets. I will discuss more about this and training in general in the new chapter I have added for 2018 called "Training".

Spraying is a continuously developing field and I am still learning, because of this I have decided to update the book every year. Like pruning a growing tree, I will attempt to remove any old and out of date branches and add new and growing ones.

What have I added into the 2019 version of the book?

Well I have put some of the comments that people have made about the book at the start, I have also included a chapter on pricing. The reason for this is that if you change the way that you work and start spraying then you also need to change the way you price to reap the full benefit of your new approach. I am working on a full book to cover this topic but for now I have included a chapter to give you some ideas to start you off.

What have I added or changed for 2020 version of the book?

I have updated the sprayer section to show some of the manufacturers updated sprayers. I have also edited some of the pictures so that they are bigger and fill the page.

Welcome to the "Updated for 2020" version of the book I hope you find it useful.

Chapter 1 - Introduction

This book is about spraying for decorators. It is aimed mainly at the professional decorator who would like to use spraying to improve productivity, achieve a first-class finish and let's face it, make more money.

The book is also aimed at the decorating student who may be studying on a full-time course or an apprentice who attends college part time.

This book covers all aspects of airless spraying on the Painting and decorating Level 3 syllabus. I am not going to look at automotive spraying or spraying outside the decorating industry although a lot of the principles are the same.

To give you an idea where the inspiration came from to write this guide, I will tell you a little about my back ground and what has brought me to the point where I am sat at a computer trying to put together a useful and entertaining guide to spraying.

I am a decorator and I have been in the trade all my life. I started out at a local company in the North West of England and I was fortunate enough to work for a company that carried out all aspects of decorating work.

The jobs ranged from large commercial decorating work including schools, hospitals, banks and churches to small domestic work such as wallpapering a hallway landing and stairs in a domestic house.

The company employed about twenty five decorators. All the skilled employees were time served decorators and were fully qualified. (In those days Advanced Craft in Painting and Decorating.) Within the team of decorators at the company there were specialists in the various skills within decorating.

There were the paperhangers, probably about 6 of these. They arrived at the job and all the preparation had been done. The ceilings were emulsioned and the woodwork was glossed. They just wallpapered the walls and then left for the next wallpapering job. This meant that they were wallpapering most of the time and therefore got to the stage where they were fast and could produce a professional first class job.

There were the church specialists; their skills involved setting up the scaffold in the church, working quickly with emulsion paint to achieve a professional job.

There was one sign writer who would carry out any lettering work on the church jobs or sign write the vans when we got new ones or repaint the statues that are found in Catholic churches.

There were also general decorators who did mainly painting on a range of work.

Finally, there were the sprayers, at my company there were two sprayers. These guys did a range of spraying work including something called Portaflek (Google this, it looks quite good and was very hardwearing) which was a multicolour spray finish.

Interestingly the sprayer was the only one with a brand-new car, I remember this because when I worked with him, he always let me drive, which was amazing for someone who had just passed their test at seventeen.

In those days we used conventional spray equipment with a compressor and spray gun. Although airless systems were available, we did not use them.

I worked for this company until my early twenties and then I set up my own business and continued to carry out decorating work but now it was all down to me.

Getting the work, pricing, sourcing materials, getting the money in. Wow and I thought my boss just played golf all day while we grafted. There was more to this business lark than first met the eye.

Business was going reasonably well when I got the opportunity of a lifetime. The job as a lecturer teaching Painting and Decorating at a local college came up.

I was twenty seven at the time, married, mortgage and kids (you get the picture). It was a job I had always fancied, let's face it, no climbing ladders, just walk around the workshop telling students what to do, it had to be a doddle of a job and I got 16 weeks holiday as well! This was just a temporary one-year post and I got through the interview and got the job.

Suddenly, I was the font of all knowledge in the eyes of the students. Of course, in reality I was far from it. I dug out my old notes from when I was an apprentice, took some books home and tried to get up to speed.

There was a lot I didn't know and in those days, I didn't like to admit that I didn't know. The students didn't just do as they were told, they were hard work. They would give me the run around and run circles round me. They must have seen the "new teacher" a mile off and taken advantage. (Hey, we were all young once, I did the same with my teachers.) This teaching lark was hard.

One old hand at the teaching job took me to one side and said. "Don't worry Pete, three or four years and it will start to get easier". Four years! I was starting my apprenticeship all over again.

Anyway, you will be glad to know that I got better at handling the students and my knowledge of the trade deepened and my confidence grew. Over the years I have had some great students, even the ones who gave me the run around and they have gone on to set up their own businesses and take on apprentices of their own.

This is a book about spraying, and I have not mentioned it much yet, however I wanted to set the scene so that you know where I have come from and a bit about my journey down the spraying road.

Many people ask me when I say that I teach decorating at college. "What do you teach the students?"

The course covers many aspects of decorating as well as "core" subjects such as health and safety, the students learn about preparation of surfaces, different primers and fillers, applying paint by brush roller and spray, wallpapering, decorative treatments such as rag rolling and marbling.

I was confident teaching most of the syllabus however when it came to spraying, I did not have very much knowledge or experience. Ok I had worked with the sprayer at work, but my foreman did all the setting up, all I did was pull the trigger. If anything went wrong, I was clueless. In the early days we just looked at conventional spraying, compressors and spray guns.

Every four or so years the syllabus changes, new items are added, some are removed, emphasis change. The basic information generally stays the same. Two new subjects were added to the syllabus: - HVLP spraying and airless spraying.

The department splashed out and bought a new HVLP system (a Wagner CS9100) and an airless system (a Wagner EP2300). We also already had a Wagner Finish 106 which is a diaphragm pump rather than a piston pump.

Wagner Finish 106 Airless (Diaphragm pump)

Wagner EP2300 Airless (Piston Pump)

Wagner CS9100 HVLP (High Volume Low Pressure)

At this point I had a bit of a problem. I had never used a HVLP system (although it was similar to the conventional guns I was used to) and I had not a clue about airless systems. I had to stand in front of the class and be the expert.

"No problem" I thought "I can manage, what could go wrong?" Well everything could go wrong, I was about to enter a steep learning curve.

My first class was with the HVLP system. HVLP stands for "High Volume Low Pressure" This is the system that the level 2 students learn about. The turbine sounds a bit like a hoover. (The original technology is based on a vacuum cleaner.) The gun is a pretty conventional suction feed gun with a cup that contains the paint below the gun.

We were using acrylic eggshell to spray a door. This worked quite well however it was very slow, and the gun kept blocking. I found out later that someone had borrowed the gun for a bit of DIY spraying at home and had not cleaned it out properly.

My first class with the airless sprayer was even more eventful. You have got to remember that this equipment had been sat unused for a while.

I had a quick lesson off my technician who had set the system up for me and I was away, full teacher mode; -

"This system is called airless because there is no air involved, the paint is pumped under high pressure to the gun where it atomises"

Sounded good so far. I switched the machine on and it made a quiet purring noise, I was using the old diaphragm system, the brand new EP2300 was in the back of the store gathering dust.

However, I could not get the system to work. After about half an hour I discovered that there is a little ball bearing that if it gets stuck (it regularly does) then that means that the pump cannot prime.

Take two, ball bearing now free, the pump is primed, and it is time to spray. I turned the prime valve to spray. I pointed the gun to the wall and pulled the trigger. Nothing. Mmm. Give the students a break at this point, they are getting a bit restless. I can sort it out while they are gone.

While the students were gone the prime valve started to leak paint on the workshop floor and things went from bad to worse. I thought "I know I will use the new machine."

We wheeled this out.

This looked complicated. After my morning so far, I decided that I needed help. Not the psychiatric type but help from the supplier - Wagner.

During the week I contacted Wagner, and they sent 2 guys down to have a look at our equipment and help me out. The little Wagner Finish 106 needed a new prime valve, I was given the name of a local company who could mend the system.

Next the gun was taken apart to reveal that the filter was solid with paint and there was no way it would have sprayed. We ordered some new filters. We ordered a new gun too, I was on a roll.

Next, they took me through the working of the big EP2300 sprayer. It was actually fairly straight forward and more like the equipment that the apprentices would come across on site.

The week after I had a successful lesson with the new sprayer. I was flying at this point, I felt like I knew all there was to know about airless spraying. Thanks to the team at Wagner we were back on track.

A couple of years later we were contacted by Dulux as they were offering a spraying course covering both airless spraying and HVLP. This was run by a chap called Peter Doyle. This was an excellent course and we all learned a great deal, I realised how little I actually knew and went on to pass all this new knowledge onto the students.

One of the things I remember from the Dulux course is that they did a study in a building to measure the difference between spraying and rolling.

On one side of the corridor decorators worked on the room in a conventional way using brushes and rollers and on the other side of the corridor they used a spraying system. You can read about this on their website.

http://www.duluxdecoratorcentre.co.uk/instore/spray_po int/spray_vs_roller.jsp

The outcome was that spraying was faster and cheaper than conventional methods. This story stuck with me and I always wanted to test this for myself. Little did I know that in a few years I would get my chance.

Since my faltering start, I have taught the use of both HVLP and airless systems for many years. The students quickly overcome the fear of using the equipment and can produce some excellent results. I have developed projects for the students to do and now when I am teaching the students how to use the airless system we mask and spray a whole room, ceiling, walls and woodwork.

We have just recently bought a new Wagner airless sprayer, this is PS3.20, a small but very handy sprayer. I have found this to be really easy for the students to use, it's light and quiet and it is very affordable.

One of the reasons I have bought this new machine is that I wanted students to see that you can buy a sprayer for under a £1000 which is very versatile. I also wanted a more modern machine as the EP2300 was a bit dated to say the least. I still use the EP2300 once in a while but tend to get the little Wagner out most weeks.

Having always enjoyed using the spray equipment I began to consider the idea of taking on some spraying contracts and getting some real world experience. I felt that this would give me some stories to tell the students and also take my skills up a level.

During the summer holidays I had the opportunity to fulfil this wish. A friend of mine has his own decorating company and he had just landed a contract to redecorate a number of student apartments.

Because I had been going onto him about the benefits of spraying, he was willing to give it a go. Having said this, he had a lot of reservations, these were,

1. spraying uses a lot of paint
2. the masking process is really slow
3. the overspray goes everywhere
4. the equipment will let you down
5. you can't touch it up
6. and "I am sure it would be better to just roll them"

I am going to return to some of these reservations later, I can understand where they come from, however in the hands of an experienced contractor all of these reservations can be overcome.

I registered as self-employed, got my very own UTR number and I was ready to go.

I was both nervous and excited when the time came to actually spray the apartments. To set the scene there were fifty apartments.

Ten rooms on each floor.

Five floors.

Each floor had two wings, each with a corridor and kitchen. So basically, ten bedrooms (with ensuite bathrooms) two kitchens (quite big) and two corridors.

I was spraying the first coat on the ceiling and walls and then finishing the ceiling. The final coat on the walls was going to be rolled. I never convinced the boss that we could touch up hence the final coat applied with a roller.

There was a preparation team who were also masking. Once that team got a floor ahead of me, I started to spray. The process went really well. After a week and I was into the swing of it and I was completing a whole floor in a day.

Yes, that's ten bedrooms, two kitchens and two corridors on my own. I was using about one hundred and twenty litres a day.

This was a success.

Visions of a BMW M3 were going around in my mind.

I was back to college full time in September, so the work took a back seat. Now a little more background information is needed here to understand my motivations for the next move.

The UK government under the guise of austerity cuts had been cutting the FE college sector budget year after year. Not just at my college but all over the country. My college had a big cut and since the bulk of the college budget is spent on staffing costs, a cut means lots of redundancies.

The workload for the remaining staff was getting unmanageable. My current role was as a manager for all the apprentices in the department (and we had a lot), I was also teaching most of the time too.

Because of this and other factors I decided to take a big pay cut, drop the management role and go part time leaving me free to pursue my paint spraying business dream.

I borrowed a sprayer from a friend until I had enough money to buy my own, had some business cards printed and I was on my way.

Work has come in at a steady pace, and I have now completed a number of airless spraying jobs. The fast and flawless finish is what customers really want. Even the woodwork can be sprayed, and the finish is great.

There are several companies who already use spraying systems to carry out decorating work however most decorators are very small companies or sole traders. I have spoken to many of these and the view of spraying is the same – sceptical.

I will give you a real-world example of this.

One of my students was painting a door at college. He was making a fantastic job of it and he was quick too. I commented on this and he told me that he was working on a building site painting new houses.

He has been undercoating doors all week, so he was getting pretty good at them. He went on to say that he had timed himself and one side of a door took him twenty minutes. There were twelve doors in the house. So that's twenty four sides, three sides per hour, eight hours to do all the doors (one coat) two days to undercoat and gloss the doors.

The apprentice had done all this maths for me which was quite impressive. We decided to try spraying a door to see how long it took. This would be ok on site because there would be no carpets or furniture to sheet up. It took thirty seconds to spray one side of a door. OK so let's say we had to mask the hinges and take the door handle off and then spray. That took four minutes.

Round this up to five minutes per side, that would mean twelve doors both sides, two coats would take a morning. *Wow that's four times faster*. That's just the doors, not the ceilings and walls. I suggested that the student mentioned this to his boss, and I offered to spend a day on site to show him how much faster we could work.

A week later the student was in college, I asked him what his boss had said. "Oh no he said he will stick to brushes and rollers because sprayers break down and you get overspray too"

Stop and think about that for a second.

Let's say his boss got paid £700 per house for labour. I know this will vary, I have actually just made the figure up. Let's say a house takes a week. That means if the sprayer is four times faster, his boss could be paid £2800 per week. If the sprayer breaks down, he could afford to buy a new one every week and still make more money.

In the States painters earn a lot more money than painters in the UK. I mean they earn two or three times more, not just a bit. The reason is that they use spraying equipment much more than we do.

A team of painters will complete the outside of a house in a day or two and charge $5000 to $7000 dollars for this depending on the size. American houses have much more to paint too not just the "trim" and are much bigger on average than ours.

Of course, it's not just all about the money, although sadly most things seem to be. Spraying gives you an easier more pleasant working day and the finish is really good.

This is why I want to write this guide, to raise awareness in the trade and to act as a reference for students studying decorating.

Another reason is that I have found when researching for my lessons that the information already out there is very dull, information is presented in tables that are difficult to understand and some information is conflicting.

I want to present the information in a way that is easy to understand. I am going to do this by telling stories that illustrate a point. Some of these stories are true and some are made up and some are a mixture of both.

On a final note.

Imagine if you bought a new car.

You arrive at the showroom and you see that they have applied the paint with a roller.

Why have they done that?

It looks terrible.

When you ring the manufacturer, he says "Well we would spray the cars, but the equipment can sometimes break, and you get overspray you know."

Would you buy the car?

Spraying is the future of decorating houses.

Sooner or later all houses will be done this way.

Decorators will earn a good living and houses will have a flawless finish. The good thing is the future could be now if you want it to be.

Chapter 2 - Training

Education and training have always been something close to my heart. I enjoyed doing my apprenticeship and going to college. Once I had completed my apprenticeship, I went back to college to do a sign writing course. I worked on the tools for ten years before I started teaching at college.

The teaching environment is a whole new ball game. It took me a long time to fully get my head around how the system works, registering students on a course, delivering the course in a way that was not too fast and not too slow. Making sure that the bright ones were kept interested while the students that struggled felt supported and not left behind.

What I didn't realise until many years later is that I was slowly falling out of touch with what was going on in the trade. It was only when I went part time and started decorating again that I realised how many gaps I had in my knowledge.

I think this is the same for all of us. We all get set in our ways, we like to think that our way is the "right" way and we have nothing more to learn. This is human nature, we are reluctant to change and learning something new, and updating your skills is definitely "change".

I have always wanted to set up my own training academy for decorators, even in my early to mid-twenties. Back then it seemed like a massive under taking and the few friends I spoke to about it seemed to think it was not a realistic goal. Once I was back on the tools, I had one or two enquires for onsite training, teaching decorators how to use airless spray equipment.

This was the simplest way for me to get into training because I didn't need a workshop or classroom or facilities. I could turn up on site and teach. This method works reasonably well.

However, for decorators who have no experience in spraying I think it is limited. Any given job only has a certain number of surfaces to learn on. When you are on a real job you cannot really take your time to explain concepts or demonstrate the right or wrong way to do things. The job has to get completed and it has to be right.

When it comes to spraying woodwork, a beginner will make quite a few mistakes. This is fine in a training workshop, but you cannot do this on site. I think the best approach is to first spend some time in a training workshop to get going and learn some skills. Then go out on site and practice. Onsite training would be good a couple of weeks after the course to further the decorator's skills and make sure that they are on track.

Although having my own training facility was the ideal, these things come at a high cost. You also have to set up the workshop and classroom with work bays and desks. None of these things come cheap.

Despite these challenges I found a unit that was a perfect space for a training workshop. It also had a room that would be ideal as a classroom area. The workshop space was being used as a storage area for a local decorator and needed to be cleared and smartened up a little before you could invite people in to learn.

While I was contemplating this workshop, I was contacted by a company based near London who were interested in coming up to Preston after Christmas and doing some training. I confidently replied that I could accommodate his decorators and booked them in for the second week in January 2017.

This was a little scary if I am honest. I had not negotiated use of the space and it needed some work doing before it was ready. There was no heating in the workshop and the course was booked for January.

The good thing was that I had already developed some training materials for the work I had been doing at local colleges. So, I had a useable training manual that I could give them, and I also had a course outline for the day that I knew worked because I had taught it a few times. I also had a presentation that I could use for the classroom part of the day.

The training workshop was going to be rented from a friend of mine who is also a decorator. I rang him about the booking, and we planned when we were going to clear the space and get organised. His lads managed to clear a lot of the paint and equipment from the main training area so that there was just a final clear up needed. We both did this in the New Year and the workshop was starting to look like a training space.

I put up a temporary wall at both ends of the workshop (dustsheets) and I was nearly ready to go.

The decorators had booked into a hotel in Blackpool. This is about thirty minutes away from Preston. Rather than give them directions and risk them getting lost I drove up to Blackpool and picked the guys up.

Wow it was a windy day, the weather in Blackpool was not great. This was Friday morning. We drove to Preston, and I got the guys settled in the classroom area with a brew. So far so good. Now that I had met the group, I was much more relaxed.

The classroom was nice and warm, and the session went really well. I am very comfortable teaching in the classroom as you can imagine after twenty five years of doing it. We covered a lot of ground and we discussed many aspects of spraying in the real world.

Once we were done in the classroom we went into the workshop, this was about 11.30. Just to set the scene, the workshop is a high room with big steel beams. The beams had been painted many years ago in a horrible silver colour. The walls had not been painted for many years and the floor needed some TLC too. However, this is what I had and, in my mind, it was ideal because every surface needed spraying! I am not sure they saw it that way.

The other problem was that it was cold. One decorator only had a T shirt on, and he looked freezing. I brought in a couple of electric heaters, but it would be a few hours before they kicked in. Note to myself, recommend jumpers next time or sort out some heating.

I had decided that I hated the silver beams, so they were going to get sprayed. I also felt that they were a good surface to learn your technique as they were deep and long, so they would need a number of trigger on and trigger off strokes. We started spraying the beams and they were looking good.

The workshop in March – two months after the first course. Still in need of development but looking more presentable.

It didn't take long for one decorator to comment "You're just getting us to spray your unit for free, aren't you?"

This made me smile because of course technically he was right, but I have since used the walls and ceiling as training areas and it's only because it was the first course that they felt this way. In fairness to me, it is much more fun spraying something that really needs doing rather than a perfect wall. It's also really good experience. I have so many surfaces in the workshop now that I very rarely use the beams as a training exercise.

The day went well, and I think the guys had a really good day. I ran them back to Blackpool and wished them well. I have kept in contact with the company since they did the course and they have gone from strength to strength. It's a nice side benefit to running the courses in that you get to meet some really great decorators.

Once the first course was done, I felt a lot happier with the set up and how the course worked.

At this point I need to roll the clock back a couple of months to November 2016. I was a member of the Facebook forum "Spraying Makes Sense" and I had found it very useful for meeting fellow sprayers, looking at spray jobs and getting advice and also helping people and giving advice too. It is a great free learning resource. The person who set the forum up is Ian Crump. He runs the forum with his wife Lyndsey.

I had met Ian and Lyndsey at the Painting and Decorating Show in 2015. They were planning on setting up spraying courses down in London and had got themselves a stand to promote the business.

Ian didn't really know me at the time, I had messaged a few encouraging words like "The courses are a great idea Ian" and the like. I felt he was on the same page as me with the ideas he had about training decorators and helping them to "up their game", however we had never met.

During early 2016 when Ian and Lyndsey were getting their head around the enormous task of setting up a private training academy we had started chatting about the ins and outs of how you would go about this.

In November 2016 Ian and Lyndsey came up to Preston and we looked at the unit I was thinking of using and we discussed setting up a company to deliver the goods. PaintTech Training Academy was born.

The first couple of courses that I ran in January where my own because I had booked these before we formed the company. They gave me a great opportunity to road test the workshop, the classroom and the curriculum.

However, I was only running with three in a group and our model was to run with five or six in a group. The plan was to run a "beta test" course in March and invite some key people who would do the course and give us some feedback.

I needed to do some development work on the workshop before the beta day. I fitted some panels to create bays, some skirting's in the bays and painted the floor in two tone grey. I still had dust sheet walls, but it was looking more like a proper training workshop.

Beta day soon came. We had a full group of five people. These where (in alphabetical order); - Charlie Budd, Jack Frost, Scott Homson, Steve Sielski and Ron Taylor.

Tracey was going to do a buffet lunch for everyone, and everyone was going to get a certificate at the end of the day.

The day went very well, without a hitch in fact, everyone enjoyed the day. We got loads of spraying done and the buffet went down a treat. By the end of the day we were excited and exhausted. PaintTech Training Academy was born for real that day.

Ian and Lyndsey found a place to rent down in Edenbridge and then set their workshop up so that it also had bays and rooms for the students to work in.

Both centres have been busy over the months since that first course in March and both centres have gradually developed so they are a better space to train in.

We had decided right at the start that we were going to have a stand at the National Painting and Decorating show in November at the Ricoh arena. This was a distant goal when we first set it however as the months went on this became our main focus.

One of my personal influences has been "The Idaho Painter." For those of you who don't know, this is a painter who lives in Idaho, called Chris Berry who has a very popular YouTube channel. His videos are informative and inspirational. Many of the budding UK sprayers watch his videos for direction.

As part of our basic spraying course we show one such video "Spraying 2 houses in one day." This video is good for a number of reasons. It shows how productive you can be with a well organised team using airless sprayers and it also shows how fast you can mask and how little overspray you can get if you know what you are doing.

Tracey decided to message Chris on Facebook to see if he was interested in coming over to England and supporting us at the show. A couple of weeks passed with no reply (if we are honest, it was a long shot) however we got a reply. He asked us to email a proposal for consideration.

This went back and forth until we had all the arrangements made and Chris, Lisa and one of their daughters, Afton were coming over to be with us at the show. We had also arranged a visit to the college where I work on Thursday, and a course on the Friday at my academy delivered by Chris himself.

Exciting times.

The day finally came, and we drove down to Coventry on the Monday to set up at the show. Ian and Lyndsey had picked Chris, Lisa and Afton up from the airport and bought them up to Coventry. It was great to meet Chris and his family, and we all set up the stand ready for Tuesday and Wednesday.

Chris has a good relationship with Titan in the states because he uses a lot of their sprayers. Because of this he had been given some giveaways. These were Wagner machines (Wagner in Europe have the same machines as Titan in America). There was a PS 3.21 (The same as the Titan 440i), three Vector grip guns (Google these they are really cool) a Wagner Finish control 3500 XVLP and a load of HEA tips (High efficiency airless tips – new to the market).

Chris was going to do a seminar in the Casino downstairs and tickets to the Seminar were going into a draw each day for a winner for the guns and on the Wednesday for a winner for the Airless sprayer. We were going to give away the last gun and XVLP sprayer on the course on Friday.

Tuesday morning at the show was very busy! We only had a little stand, but we were drawing big crowds! Tickets for the seminar with Chris sold like hot cakes.

Ian did a master class for Tikkurila and I did a master class for PaintTech Training Academy. Both were bursting at the seams and went really well with lots of interest and questions afterwards.

Chris did his seminar at 4:00pm and it was brilliant! The hour over ran but no-one seemed to mind. We raffled off the Vector grip gun and one happy decorator took it home with him.

Wednesday was a little quieter but still busy, 4:00pm soon came around and we were packing up, the arena quickly emptied, and we were on our way home.

Thursday brought with it a lie in. Luxury, after a few very busy days it was nice to have a little break. We were going to be taking Chris around a college on the Thursday. In America there is nothing like the colleges we have in the UK for decorating.

We take for granted the fact that we can go to college (for free in most cases) and learn a trade and come out qualified. This qualification can then be used anywhere in the world to get a job. One of the goals Chris has is to set up a Paint Life Academy in Idaho so that people can train to be painters properly.

The trip around college was an eye opener for him I think, meeting the students, looking at the workshops and classroom. This is training on a multimillion pound scale and is quite a set up. We train approximately 300 apprentices each year across all the construction trades.

In the afternoon we went to our Preston Academy to set up for the course on Friday and for Chris to see the facility and get comfortable with it.

We had twenty people coming for a day course with Chris. The morning was going to be in our brand new café style classroom and then after a large buffet lunch we were going into the workshop to have a go at spraying with a large extension pole among other things.

I have never had twenty people in the workshop, so we were pushing the boundaries a little. Fingers crossed for a good day.

Chris in our new classroom

Friday came, everyone arrived and got settled in the classroom area. Chris got into his presentation and before long it was lunch time!

The buffet lunch was awesome, one of our attendees from Preston had provided a large selection of delicious American themed cakes for free (Alison Sielski) and Tracey of course had done a top class buffet.

The afternoon went really well, we all had a go at spraying with extension poles longer than we had ever done before, and we had a go at spraying woodwork too with the guidance of Chris. It was amazing to see "live" some of the things we have all seen him do in his videos.

I think this sums up the whole day

On a final note, we had two decorators come over from Belgium. This is quite a trip. One of these guys won the XVLP sprayer and went home very happy.

What will be the future of training for Decorating?

I think we have an exciting future ahead. A whole new class of decorator is emerging, who is trained in the latest methods and products. This means that work can be done more productively, and the decorator can ultimately have a better work life.

If you are reading this book, then I assume that you are interested in spraying and working smarter in your business. If you have not done a course but want to learn more (for free) then check out "The Idaho Painter" on YouTube, there are loads of spraying videos on there to get you started.

Chapter 3 - Types of sprayers

There are many different spray systems on the market. There are different types of sprayers and different manufacturers. To simplify things here are the 3 main types of spray systems.

1. Conventional
2. HVLP
3. Airless

Conventional spray systems

A conventional spray set up has a compressor which produces compressed air, the gun is attached to this using an airline. The gun has a paint container attached to it and the combination of air flowing through the gun mixed with the paint produces a spray.

Conventional spray systems are used widely in many industries and produce a very high quality of finish. They are mainly suited to being used in a spray booth or workshop situation due to the compressor being quite heavy and difficult to transport.

Many decorators do however use conventional compressor set ups on site, the advantages are the fine finish and the relatively low purchase cost. The disadvantage can be increased overspray due to the higher pressures (compared to HVLP) that they spray at.

An electric compressor

The compressor draws air into a tank where it is compressed to a higher pressure than the air in the room. This air is stored in the tank until it is needed by the spray gun. The air hose runs from the compressor to the gun.

A conventional spray gun

This is a gravity feed spray gun. (Picture next page). The paint is in the litre sized pot attached to the top of the gun. Paint is fed into the air stream by gravity. The air hose is attached to the handle.

When the trigger is pulled air passes through the gun and the paint is drawn into the spray tip. Air passes through the two horns on the air cap and this atomises the paint.

The flow of paint can be controlled by a knob on the back of the gun, this controls how far back the fluid needle is pulled and therefore how much paint is allowed through the spray tip.

Another type of gun is suction feed gun. As the name suggests this allows paint to flow using suction to draw the paint up into the stream of air.

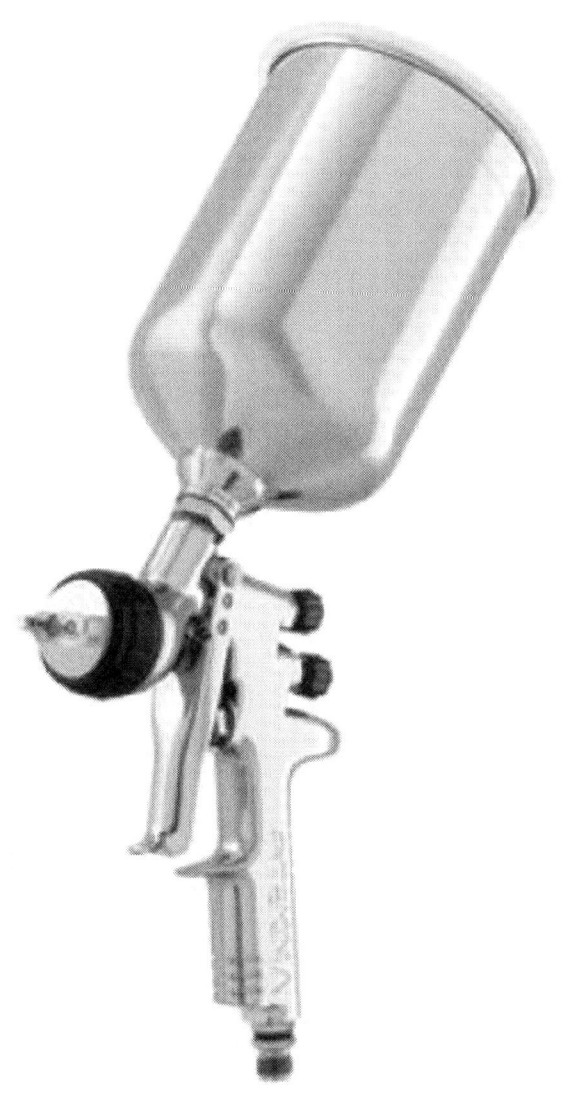

A gravity feed gun

The advantage of both these types of gun is that they are easy to clean out as the paint is contained in a small container as part of the gun.

The disadvantage is that the container only holds about a litre a paint and also the gun cannot be turned upside down.

To remedy both these problems you can use a pressure pot. This is a separate container which contains the paint.

Some pressure pots are quite large, and you can put a whole 5 litre tin of paint into the pot and feed from that. The pressure pot is attached to the gun via a hose.

The gun has a hose running to the pressure pot and a hose running to the compressor. The pressure pot also has a hose running to the compressor.

The gun is a lot lighter because there is no paint container attached and the gun also can be turned upside down or sprayed at any angle.

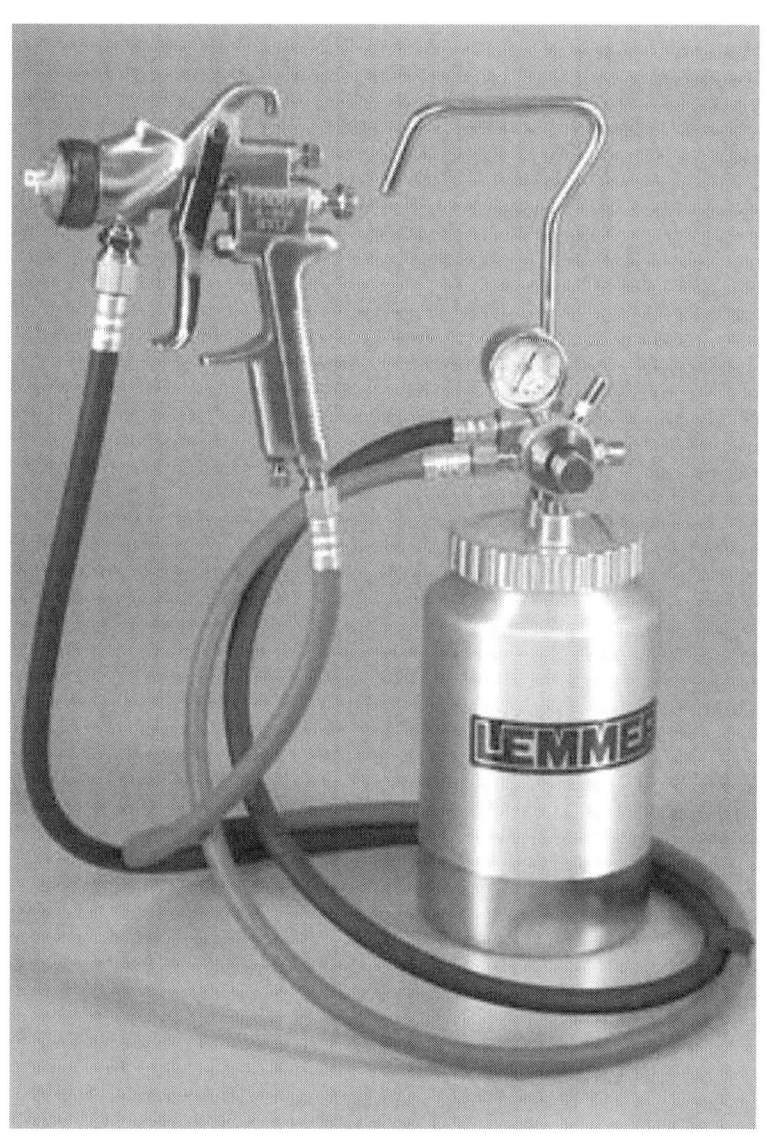

Pressure pot and gun.

High Volume Low Pressure Turbine systems

Unlike conventional spray systems, a HVLP turbine system utilises a lightweight air turbine rather than a large air compressor to supply the air to atomise the paint. Being lightweight they are highly portable and won't break your back carrying them around site!

With HVLP the air is supplied at a much lower pressure which means that the amount of overspray is substantially reduced. To compensate for the lower pressure (LP) these systems supply a higher volume (HV) of air to atomise the paint.

HVLP turbine systems can be used with a wide range of decorative and industrial coatings including wood stains, varnishes and finish paints such as gloss and eggshell.

The smaller models are also very popular as "spray tan" applicators bought by end users and professional tanning salons.

HVLP guns are also available for a compressor set up however the fittings are different, and they cannot be used on a turbine. I am going to explore these systems more in a future book "Fast and Flawless Fine Finishing."

A Wagner HVLP turbine, air hose and gun

The turbine is basically a vacuum cleaner running in reverse so that instead of sucking up air it blows out air. The original HVLP systems where spray guns attached to a vacuum cleaner. The advantage of HVLP systems is that they do not store compressed air in a tank (which can be dangerous) and also because the air is at such a low pressure there is not as much overspray as a conventional system.

The equipment is lightweight and can easily fit into the back of your car. It is also easily stored in your garage or under the stairs. HVLP systems can be used to spray smaller areas such as doors, radiators, staircase spindles and skirting.

The finish is good, and the spray pattern can be adjusted to suit the surface being sprayed. The spray pattern can even be changed to spray a circle which is great for spindles on stairs.

The main disadvantage of HVLP is that it is quite slow. This is not a problem if you are only spraying your front door but if you wanting to spray 30 panel doors both sides then it could get quite tedious.

XVLP (eXtra Volume Low Pressure)

A new generation of turbines has been developed to improve on the advantages that HVLP offers. This new technology covers a much wider spectrum than today's HVLP technology, and it offers the special Extra (X).

Due to 60% higher air volume and 30% greater area coverage than other low-pressure devices the XVLP series shows a higher atomisation performance.

The XVLP guns are faster and have a wider spray width. They are however just as controllable and make it easier to change colours over while working. As you can see from the picture they look pretty cool too.

There is a handheld version of this available too which is the Finish 3500. I have used one of these and I found it quite versatile.

Airless spraying systems

Airless systems are made up of a pump, fluid hose and spray gun. The big difference with an airless system compared to the others we have looked at is that there is no compressed air involved. In fact, there is no air involved at all, hence "airless".

The paint is pumped under very high pressure (approximately 2200 psi) down a hose to the gun. The gun is basically a tap on the end of the hose allowing the painter to turn the flow on and off.

Part of the gun is a fluid tip, this is a small opening or orifice that turns the flow of paint from a jet to a mist. The combination of the very high pressure and the small opening causes the paint to atomise.

The big advantage of an airless system is that paint can be applied to the surface very fast. If you are painting large areas, it is possible to paint up to 200m² per hour. It is also versatile enough to apply finishing paints to the woodwork.

The disadvantage is the very high pressure which can be dangerous if not used correctly and can cause a lot of overspray. Both these limitations can be overcome however with the correct use of the equipment.

An airless sprayer

Air assisted airless

This seems to be a contradiction in terms. Airless with air. A standard airless system is not great for fine finish work such as furniture or even woodwork because it is so fast and aggressive it is very difficult to control.

Air assisted softens the jet of paint coming out of the tip and makes it more controllable.

Chapter 4 – Companies and what they offer

There are a number of companies who manufacture and supply airless spraying systems. The following is not a complete list, however these are the main players. The list is in no particular order.

I have included a selection of airless sprayers from each manufacturer with specifications for comparison and cost at the time of writing. You can research these companies yourself on the internet if you are thinking of buying a machine.

I have included four pieces of information for each sprayer. These are; -

Use, this is typically where the sprayer would be used. Some sprayers are designed for occasional use and would not be used every day. The bigger sprayers are designed for large site work and could be used daily.

Tip size, this is a very useful piece of information and gives you an indication of how powerful the sprayer is. You really need the sprayer to be able to run a tip size higher than the size you will be using the most. See the chapter on tips to get more of an idea of what this actually means. I would aim to buy a sprayer that will go up to 0.021" tip at least.

Maximum delivery, this is the amount of paint that the sprayer will spray in a minute. Some of the amounts are quite eye watering. One machine can deliver five litres a minute. That's a lot!

Finally, price. This needs no explanation. These are approximate costs at the time of writing and of course will change so check these out for yourself when you are thinking of buying a machine. Prices vary from supplier to supplier and it is worth shopping around. I have included an approx. price just so that you can compare with other sprayers in the book.

What sprayer shall I buy?

A common question decorators ask when they have decided to buy an airless sprayer is "Which one should I buy?" There is not one simple answer to this question.

The best way to understand this is to think about what you would advise someone who asked you "What first car should I buy?" There would be three factors to consider.

First and the most important is what are you going to use the car for. If you are just driving around the city and parking, then a small easy to park, cheap to run car would be a good choice. If you are doing a lot of motorway miles, then you would be better with a bigger more comfortable car.

Secondly you must consider your budget. If you have a £1000 to spend then get the best car that will do the job for that price. You may have to get a second hand car at this price even though you probably want a new one.

Finally, you may have a favourite make and model, even though many makes, and models fit the criteria set by factors 1 and 2. For example I like Fords, so I tend to advise people get a Ford Fiesta as a city run-around.

This is not necessarily the right answer, there are many makes and models in that category. It is up to the person buying to find their favourite. You do this by shopping around.

With a sprayer, you need to go through the same three steps.

1. What are you going to be using the sprayer for? If you are a DIY decorator, then you could buy a DIY spraying machine, and this would be quite cheap. If you are a professional, then you need a professional sprayer.

   How much spraying are you going to do? If you are going to spray once a week, then a smaller sprayer will do the job. If you are going to be spraying every day, then you will need a bigger sprayer.

2. Once you know what you need the sprayer for then look at the models that fit these criteria. The major players in the market are Wagner, Graco and Titan. Costs new will be fairly similar for each category of

sprayer. For example, a Wagner sprayer which is designed for spraying once a week would cost approx. £1000 new.

3. Finally decide on which brand you like the most. Only YOU can do this. People will always advise you on the machine that they own and of course they think it's the best. Make your own mind up on this. Maybe try a friend's sprayer and see if you like it. Research on the internet the different brands available.

Finally, enjoy doing the research, I always think choosing a sprayer can be more fun than actually buying. The following are some sprayers that I have already researched to start you off on your quest.

Graco

Graco are an American company and produce a good quality range of airless sprayers which are popular with decorators in both America and the UK.

Graco GXFF

This little sprayer has been designed with the decorator in mind. It is affordable and is light and easy to carry. It has a 1.5 gallon hopper which will hold enough paint to spray the typical ceiling or woodwork in a house.

I have one of these and I use it quite a bit on smaller single room spraying jobs or where I am using it as a second sprayer to do the woodwork while I use a bigger sprayer to do all the walls and ceiling.

Use; Light use, domestic decorating maybe used one or twice a week.

Max tip size is 19 thou

Max delivery is 1.5 litres per minute

Approximate cost - £700

Graco GX21

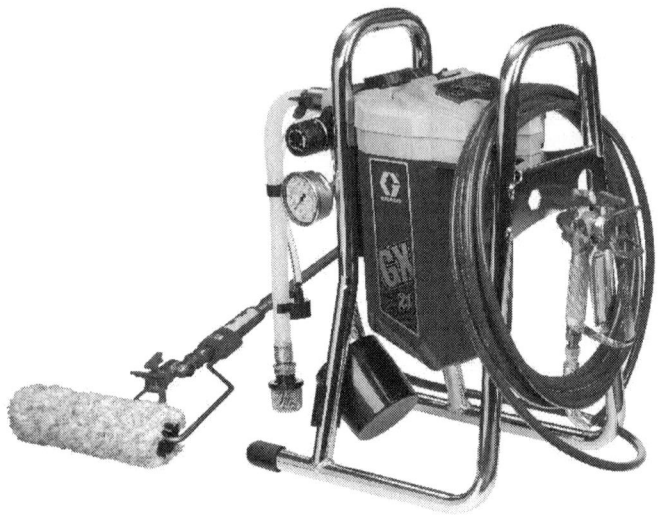

The same unit as the GXFF but with a suction feed hose instead of a hopper.

Graco Ultra and Ultramax

Graco produce a range of handheld sprayers for touching up and spraying small areas. The two cordless ones are the Ultra and the Ultramax. The Ultramax sprays both solvent and water based paints. There is also a corded version of this sprayer available.

These airless sprayers are pretty cool, and they have been very popular when launched in this country. The battery life is not great, but you can get a 5ah Dewalt battery at a reasonable cost and this will extend the working time of the sprayer.

Many decorators are buying this sprayer thinking it can be used to spray out whole houses. While it can do this there are a few things to bear in mind. The battery will spray about a gallon before running out.

The pump has a 300 litre life. This can be changed for a new pump however its shows that Graco intended the sprayer to be used for smaller areas such as doors windows, radiators and touching up.

Use, for touching up and small areas.

Maximum tip size is 16 thou.

Approximate cost is £500.

Graco 495 ST Max

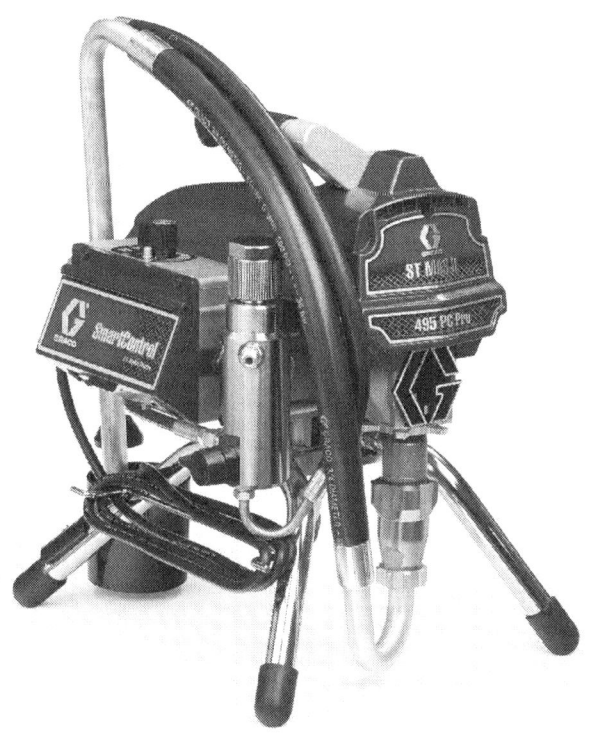

Use, this is an entry to mid-level and is quite versatile.

Maximum tip size is 25 thou.

Maximum delivery is 2.1 litres per minute.

Approximate cost is £1,700.

Graco Mark V

This is an amazing sprayer, it has been designed to spray airless plaster and intumescent materials. The pump is low down so that it can pump heavy materials with ease. It can also of course spray paint. You can easily run 2 guns off this machine.

It is quite heavy to get in and out of the van. If you are going to be spraying spray plaster all the time, then you need to invest in a hopper that goes with the Mark V. These are big enough to hold a days' worth of spray plaster, but they are quite expensive at just under a grand.

Use, this sprayer is designed for daily use and will spray plaster.

Max tip size is 39 thou (or 2 guns with 0.019").

Maximum delivery is 5.1 litres per minute.

Approximate cost is £3,000.

Titan

This is an American company who are now part of the Wagner group. They produce a range of sprayers which are very popular in America. Titans are nice looking machines, they are reliable and good to work with. The Titan 440i is one of the best-selling sprayers in America.

Titan 460e

Use, this is an entry level machine.

Max tip size is 21 thou.

Maximum delivery is 1.6 litres per minute.

Approximate cost is £1,500.

Titan 750e

Use, this is a larger machine for commercial work.

Maximum tip size is 0.027".

Maximum delivery is 2.65 litres per minute.

Approximate cost is £3000.

Q-Tech

This is a relatively new player in the market. They produce a range of sprayers from entry level up to large commercial sprayers. They are good value for money and are reliable pumps.

Q-Tech QT190

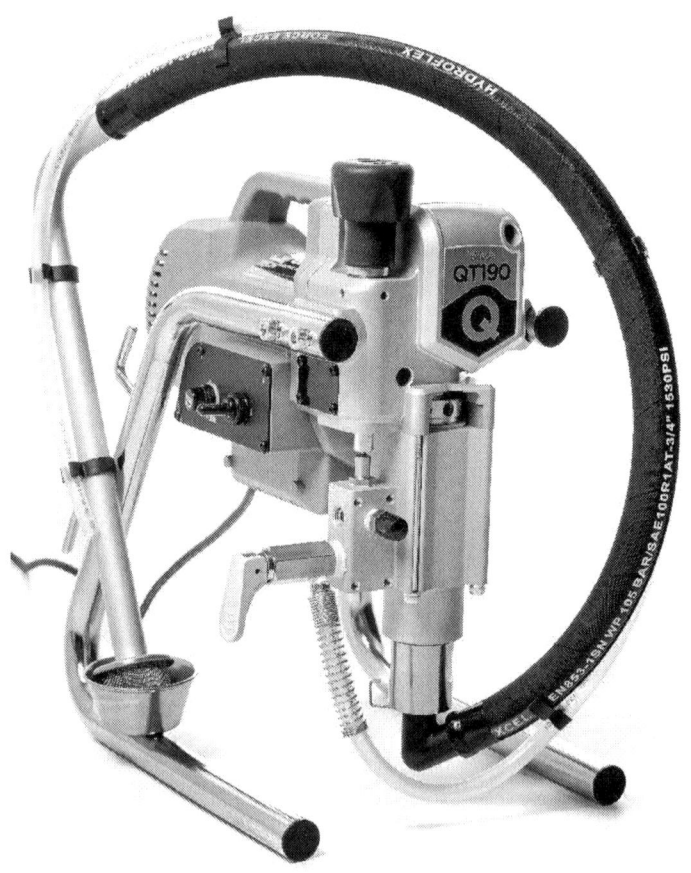

This is a great little pump and is good value too. It is a quiet little machine that can handle most domestic spraying jobs. It also comes with a Tritech gun which is pretty cool.

Use, this is an entry level machine.

Maximum tip size is 19 thou.

Maximum delivery is 1.9 litres per minute.

Approximate cost is £700.

Q-Tech QT290

I have used one of these sprayers and it is a very capable machine for the price. If you are looking for a new machine and you have a limited budget it might be worth checking these machines out. I know a few decorators who own this model and they love them.

Use, this is a mid-range sprayer.

Maximum tip size is 25 thou.

Maximum delivery is 2.9 litres per minute.

Approximate cost is £1,200.

Q-Tech QT550

Use, this is a large capacity sprayer that is designed for everyday use. It's simply a beast of a sprayer.

Maximum tip size is 31 thou.

Maximum delivery is 5.5 litres per minute.

Approximate cost is £3000.

Wagner

These are a German company who have been producing airless sprayers for many years. They offer good value for money and reliability.

All my sprayers at college have been Wagner machines and they have been very reliable and easy to use. My first sprayer I bought for my business was a Wagner too, a little PS 3.20

PS 3.20

I have owned this little sprayer for many years, and it has been a real handy machine. I have sprayed out full houses with it and I have also used it to spray single rooms. It's light and easy to transport.

Use, and entry level sprayer.

Maximum tip size is 21 thou.

Maximum delivery is 1.6 litres per minute.

Approximate cost is £900.

PS 3.21

I don't have this machine however I have a Titan 440i which is an identical machine but for the American market. It's a nice sprayer to use, a bit heavier that the PS 3.20 but more powerful.

Use, A good all-rounder.

Maximum tip size is 23 thou.

Maximum delivery is 2.0 litres per minute.

Approximate cost is £1200.

Tritech

T5

One of the most common questions that I am asked is "What sprayer do you recommend?" to which I always reply the Tritech T5.

Why is this?

I feel that it is a good all-round machine. It has aerospace grade alloys in the pump that will not rust and has a unique packing system that makes it very easy to service.

The motor is guaranteed for life which shows how confident the manufacturer is about their product. The pressure is very controllable, and you get a consistent spray pressure at the gun.

Use, a good all-rounder for the painting contractor

Maximum tip size is 25 thou.

Maximum delivery is 2.2 litres per minute.

Approximate cost is £1,700.

Tritech T11

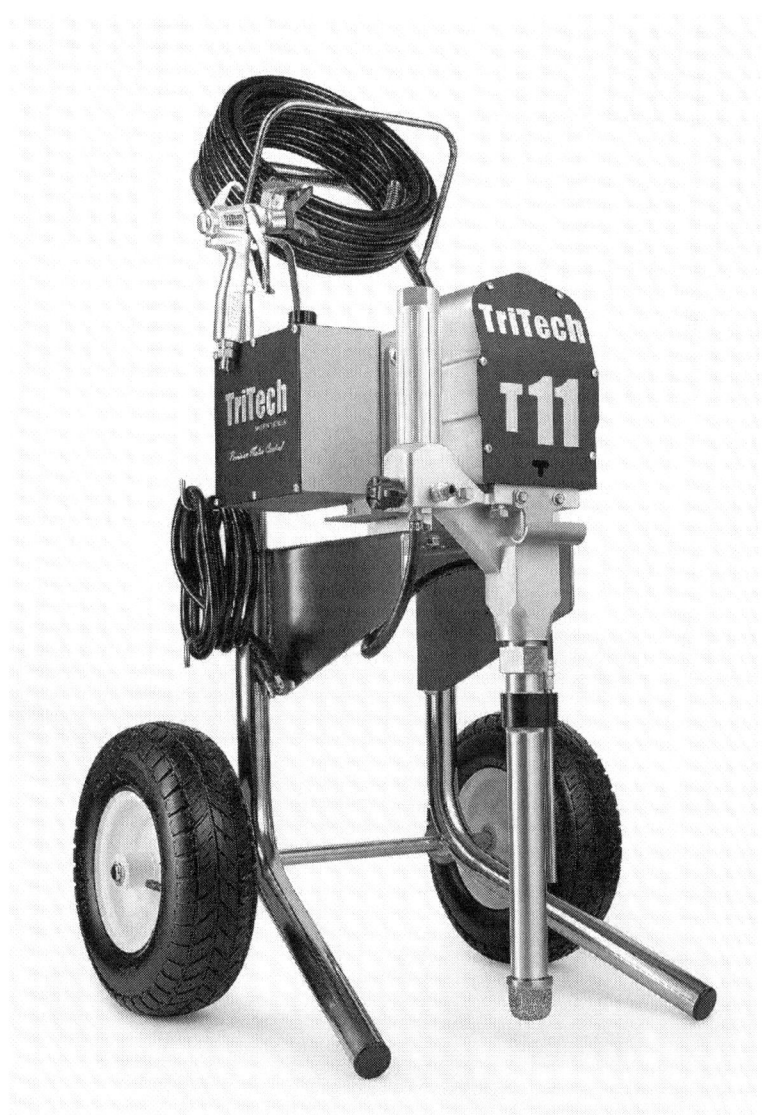

Use, currently Tritech's most powerful machine at the moment. It can spray emulsion, heavy coatings and a range of intumescent coatings

Maximum tip size is 33 thou.

Maximum delivery is 4.43 litres per minute.

Approximate cost is £3600.

I actually own a T7 which is between these two machines. Why do I not recommend the T7 when I have one? Well of course I do but the T5 will do everything you want and is nearly £300 cheaper. If you have the cash and you want a bigger capacity sprayer then of course go for it.

Chapter 5 - Essential equipment and how it works

If you have never used an airless system, it can be a little daunting when you have to use it for the first time. The first thing you need to do is familiarise yourself with the equipment and associated tools.

The airless system

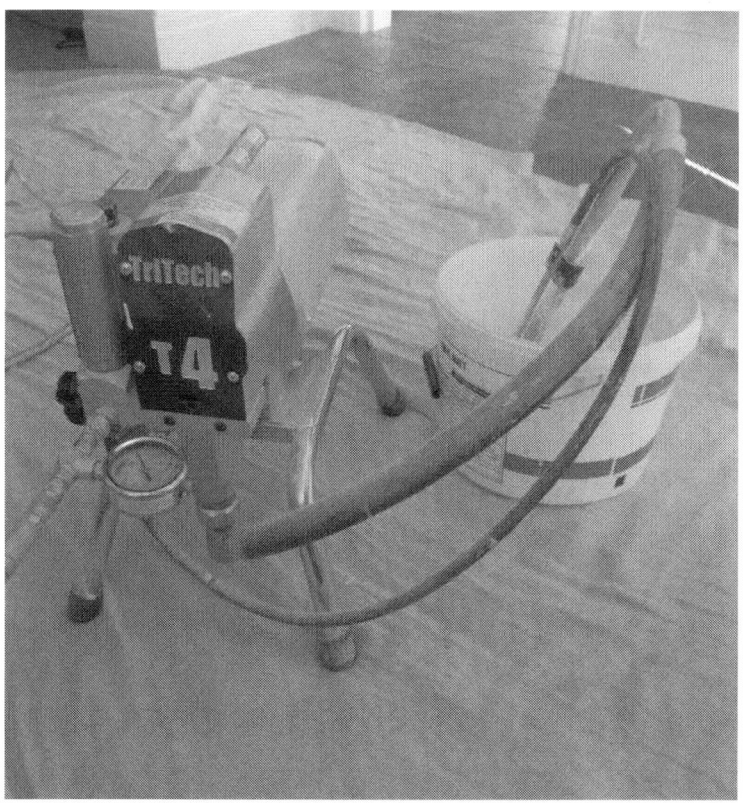

This is a picture of a complete system. This is a small Tritech T4 model, useful for spraying small projects such as domestic properties. Here the suction tube is in the paint along with the return tube.

The system is set up ready to go. We can look at each part of the system to get familiar with it.

The transformer

Electrical equipment on site runs on 110V. The electrical supply in the house is 240V this means that you need a transformer to step the current down to 110V. You can buy 240V airless systems however these cannot be used on site.

Transformers are rated. This one is a 3.3KVA. As a rule of thumb, you need your transformer to match your sprayer. If you have a 2 kW sprayer, then you need at least a 2 KVA transformer.

The pressure gauge

This is important, and you need to know what pressure that you are spraying at, some systems have a digital gauge, however here you can see a good old-fashioned gauge.

These can be bought separately and added to your sprayer between the outlet of the sprayer and the hose. Typically, you will be spraying at 2000 psi however there are a number of factors which dictate the pressure and we will discuss this in the next chapter.

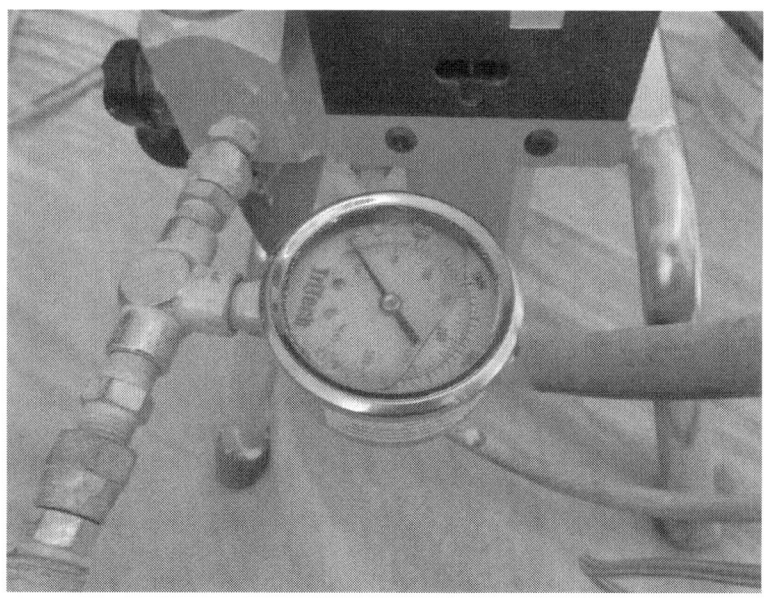

The pressure control

As the name suggests this controls the pressure. Keep this turned down to the minimum when setting up the sprayer or cleaning. Turn the control to the correct pressure when you start painting.

The spray gun

This is the part of the system that applies the paint to the wall and controls the flow of paint. We will look at a disassembled gun later on in this chapter. You can also see the tip inserted in the gun.

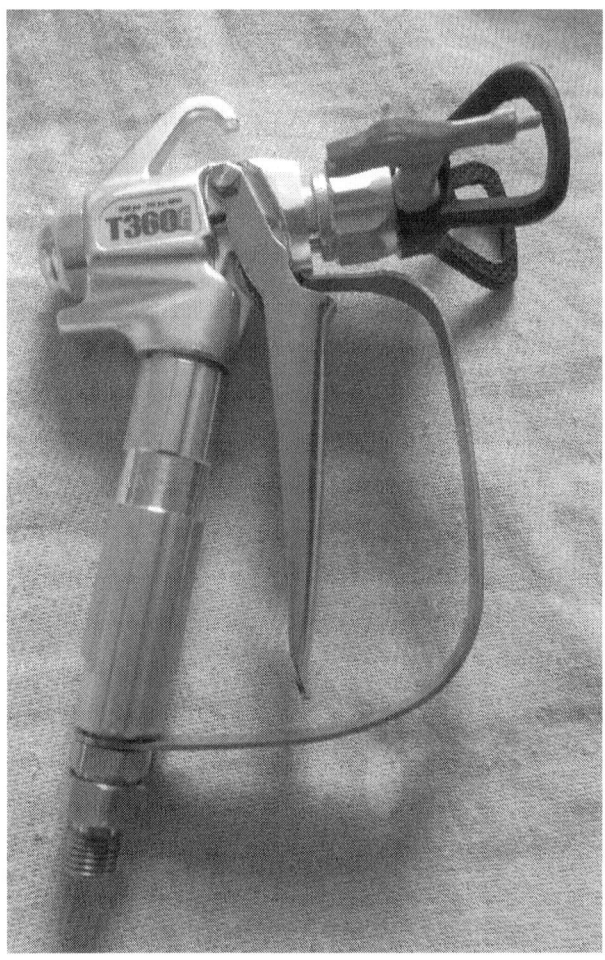

The high pressure hose

This is the hose that transfers the paint from the pump to the gun. As the name suggests it is designed to work at high pressure. Hoses are usually either 7.5m or 15m in length.

This must not have any splits or holes and should not be repaired if damaged. Be careful not to kink the hose when working and make sure that it stays uncoiled.

Easier said than done sometimes.

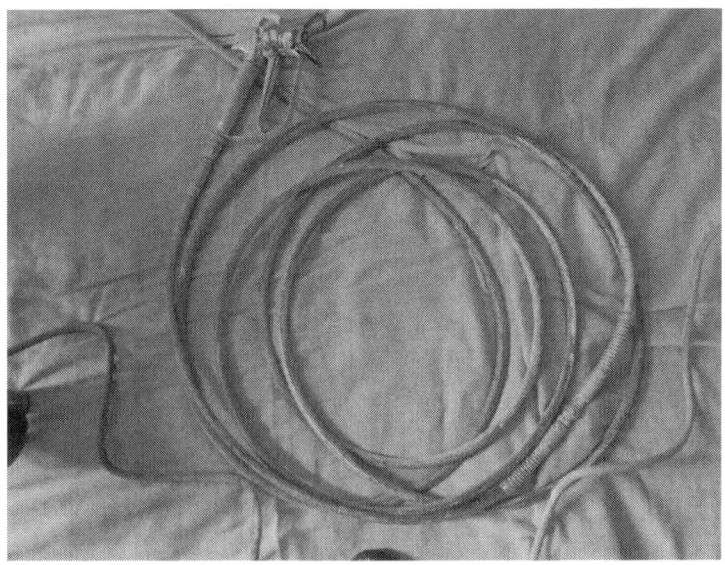

The prime/spray valve

The spray/prime valve can be set to prime (pointing down on this machine) or spray (as shown in the picture).

When the paint circulates through the pump and back into the bucket, this is when the pump is being primed.

If the paint is sent down the hose to the gun to spray, then this is spray mode.

The manifold filter

This is the filter on the spray machine itself. This must be cleaned out every time that you clean out the machine.

The filter taken off

Here you can see the filter housing has been removed for cleaning. The filter inside the housing is a 50 mesh filter. The large spring goes inside the filter to prevent it from being crushed.

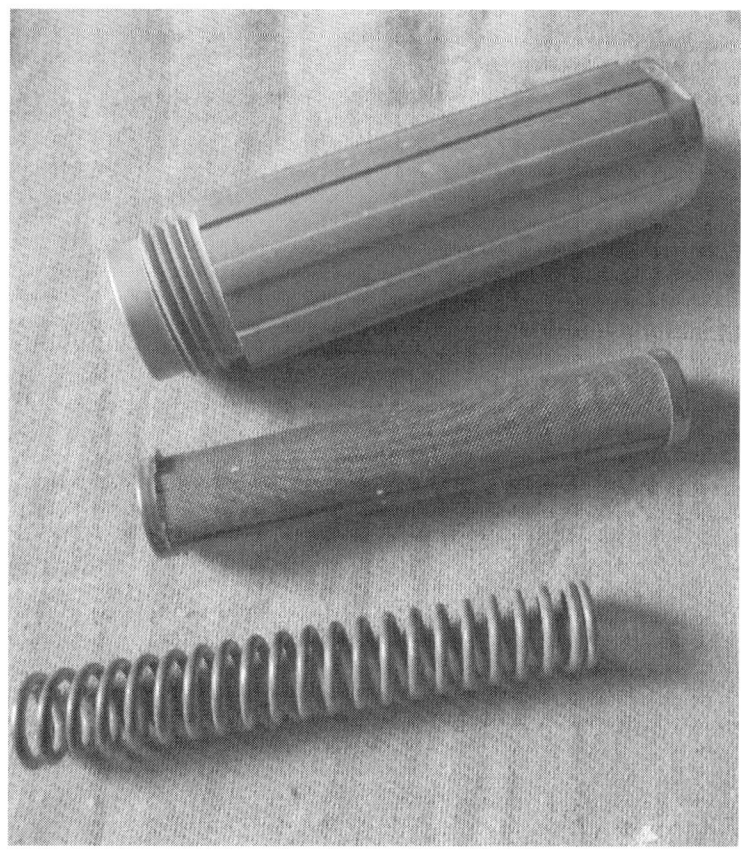

The gun extension

These can be bought in various sizes. Here you can see a 12" gun extension.

These attach onto the gun as shown and are useful for spraying ceilings as they give you more reach and also, they are useful for spraying walls as they save you from bending and stretching all the time.

They take a little getting used to but are worth the effort.

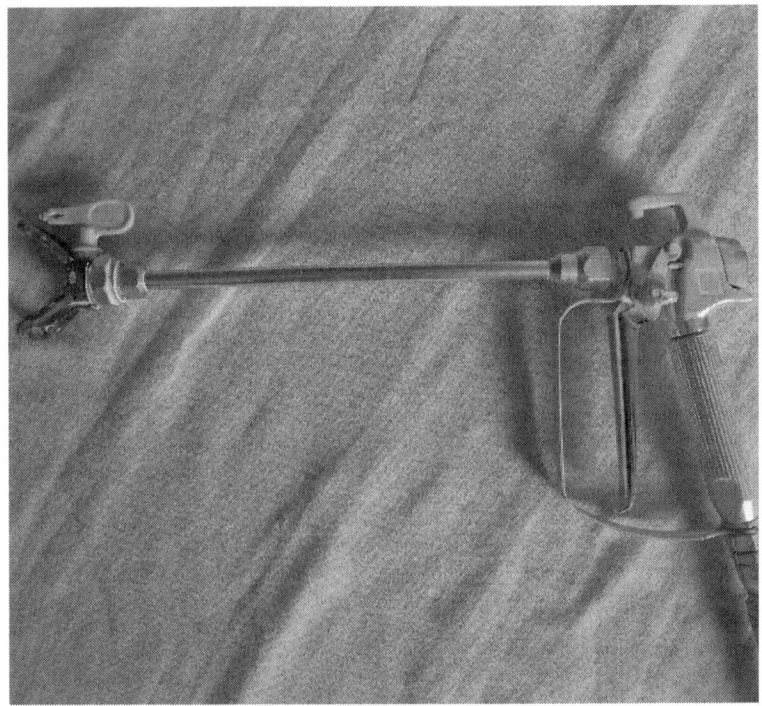

The Whip hose

This is a short flexible hose that connects onto the end of the hose. The gun then attaches to this. It is a more flexible hose which makes gun control much easier. This is worth getting and will save you a lot of arm ache.

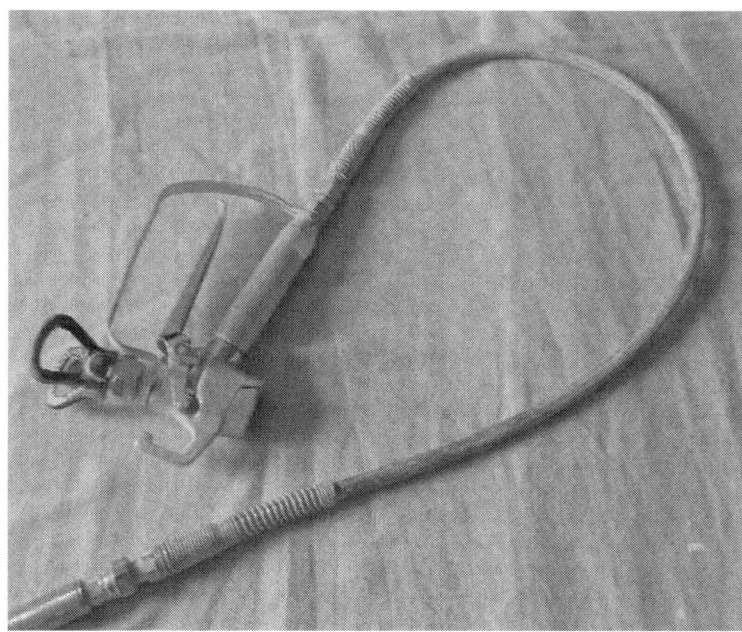

The gun taken apart

Here is the gun with the handle removed showing the filter and the tip and tip guard removed. You will need to do this when you are cleaning the gun out and if you change the tip and therefore have to change the filter.

The tip guard is to prevent you from injecting yourself with paint.

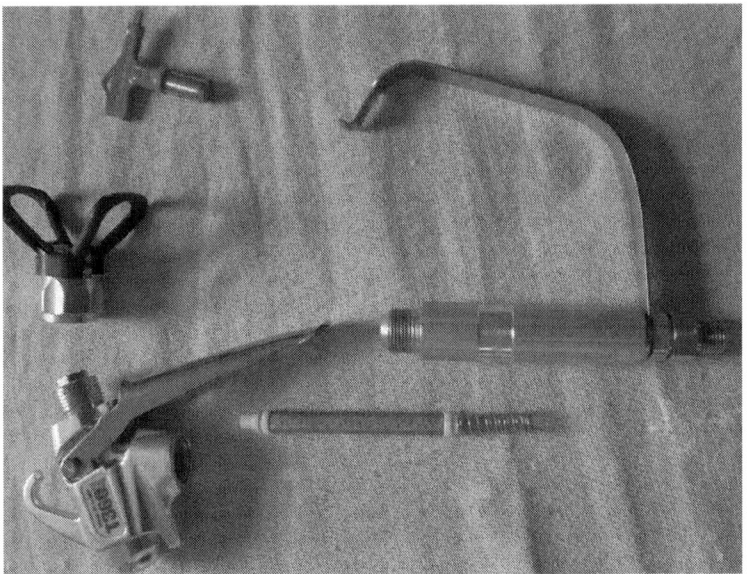

In the previous picture, you can see that the filter is removed. You can see that the filter goes into the gun one way (there is a spring on the bottom). If you accidentally put the filter into the gun the wrong way, then the gun will not work at all.

Sometimes this can be a difficult fault to trace if you don't realise that you have done this. Some filters are screw in which make it easier.

Spanners

You will need at least 2 spanners. An adjustable is also handy. These are to attach the hose to the pump and attach the gun to the hose. Most sprayers have the spanners with them when you buy one.

The tool box

You need somewhere to keep your spanners, extension poles, guns, oil, a rag etc. Saves getting to the job 50 miles away and finding that you have forgotten something.

Throat seal the pump

When the pump is in use, you will need to put throat seal onto the piston every 4 hours. The point where you do this will vary from machine to machine, but it is usually obvious. Here is where you do it on the Tritech. This is on the front of the machine.

Alternative guns.

You may not want to stick with the gun that came with the machine. The Tritech guns are good but some other sprayers may have a poor quality gun. The most guns have a standard thread for the tip guard which is 7/8".

Below is the Wagner "Vector grip" gun. Go online and have a look what is available.

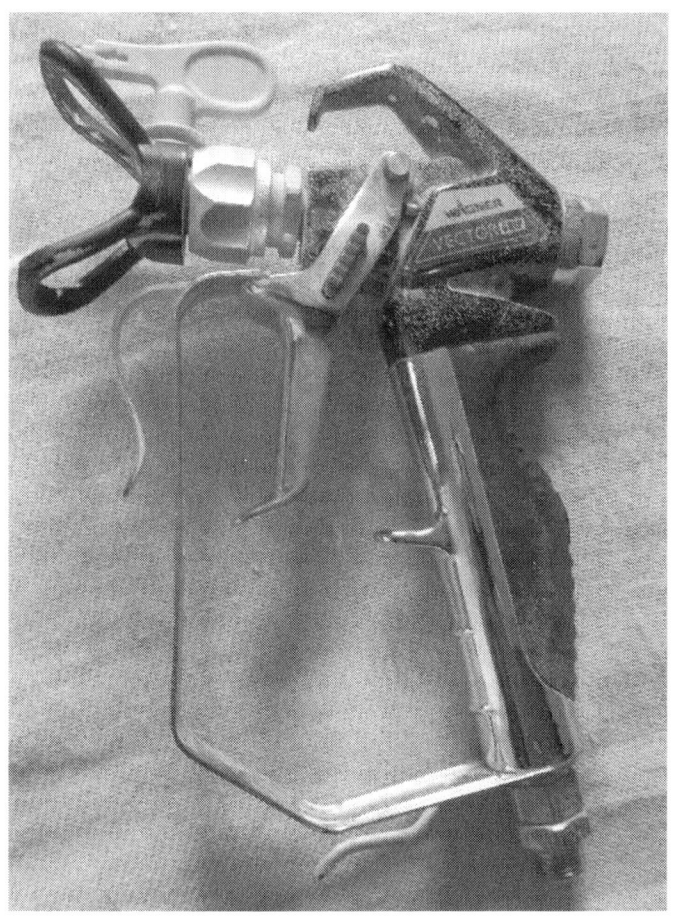

A few tips on tips

If you remove the tip from the tip guard, then all you are left with is a tap on the end of a hose. The paint will come out of the gun in a stream just like water from a hose pipe. This shows how important the tip is to the whole airless spraying process.

The picture shows a standard Wagner 517 tip for emulsion, a Wagner 208 fine finish tip and a Tritech tip. Most makes of tip will fit your tip guard except Graco who do tips slightly bigger to fit their own tip guard. You can put a Graco tip guard on your gun though because it has a standard thread.

There are a few levels of understanding when it comes to tips. If you are new to spraying and you go and do some research on the internet or a trade leaflet, then you are usually presented with a description of what the number on the tip means and a big table of paints with a recommended tip.

This however does not give you a feel for the importance of the tip or help you choose one.

Most decorators will just find a general purpose tip and stick with that one tip for years.

So, to start with let's talk about that magic number stamped on the tip and what it means. All tip manufacturers will stamp the size of the tip on the side of the plastic handle.

For example, a common tip size is 517. There are two parts to the number although it is written as one number. 5 and 17. Each number refers to a different thing.

Fan size

The 5 is the fan size. 5 means the angle the spray comes out of the gun is 50° (the bigger the angle to wider the fan). This does not mean anything to most people so to work out the actual width of the spray pattern as it hits the wall you double the number, and this will give the fan width in inches.

A 5 will give a 10" spray pattern if the gun is 12" (30cm) away from the wall.

If the gun is close to the surface, then the fan width will be smaller and if you are farther away it will be bigger.

If you are spraying a wall, then a bigger fan will put more paint on the wall and you will complete the wall faster. You can buy tips that go up to 12 (for example a 1221) this will give a fan size of 24" and cover the wall or ceiling much faster.

If you are spraying skirting's, then a fan size of 3 (for example a 310) will give a fan size of 6" which is a good width to paint the woodwork.

The fan size is pretty easy to get your head around. If you have two or three different sizes, then it is worth trying each one on a large piece of card taped to the wall.

Put the tip in and spray a good pattern on the card. Try a bit closer or farther away to get the feel for what effect this has on the width of the spray band.

I always have a bucket of clean water handy to put the tips in if I am working with more than one in the day so that the tip does not dry out before I come to clean them out later. (I also do this at brew time and dinner time).

Orifice size

The second part of the number (17 in our 517 example) is the size of the hole in the tip. The hole is very small and is measured in thousandths of an inch.

So, 17 is 17 thousandths of an inch or 17 thou. The bigger the number the bigger the hole that the paint is forced through. Forcing the paint through a tiny hole is what causes the paint to turn into a spray (or atomise).

This idea seems simple enough however it took me a while to fully understand what this means in practical terms. There are a few things to consider when you are choosing the orifice size.

1. Some paints are thicker and need a bigger hole or orifice size, some paints are thinner and will go through a smaller hole. So if you are spraying emulsion you will need to use the correct size of tip or the paint will block the tip and not spray. I will include a table of paints and orifice sizes later.

2. The bigger the hole the faster the paint will come out of the gun and the more difficult it will be to control. So, for example you might use a 517 tip (17

thou orifice size) to spray emulsion. If you are spraying a flat and previously painted wall, then you may find that the paint comes out so fast that you end up putting too much on the wall and it runs. If you are spraying a newly plastered wall which is very absorbent, then you will be ok.

To *slow the flow of paint down* and therefore put less paint on the wall with each pass you could drop down to a 515 tip (15 thou orifice size – same fan width). I sometimes actually say to the students "use a slower tip" rather than smaller tip although of course it would mean the same thing.

3. Finally, if you use a 517 tip and put 1000's of gallons through it for years it will wear out giving you a bigger orifice size than is stamped on the tip. Typically, a tip will start to wear after 250 litres of paint.

Here is a standard 517 tip

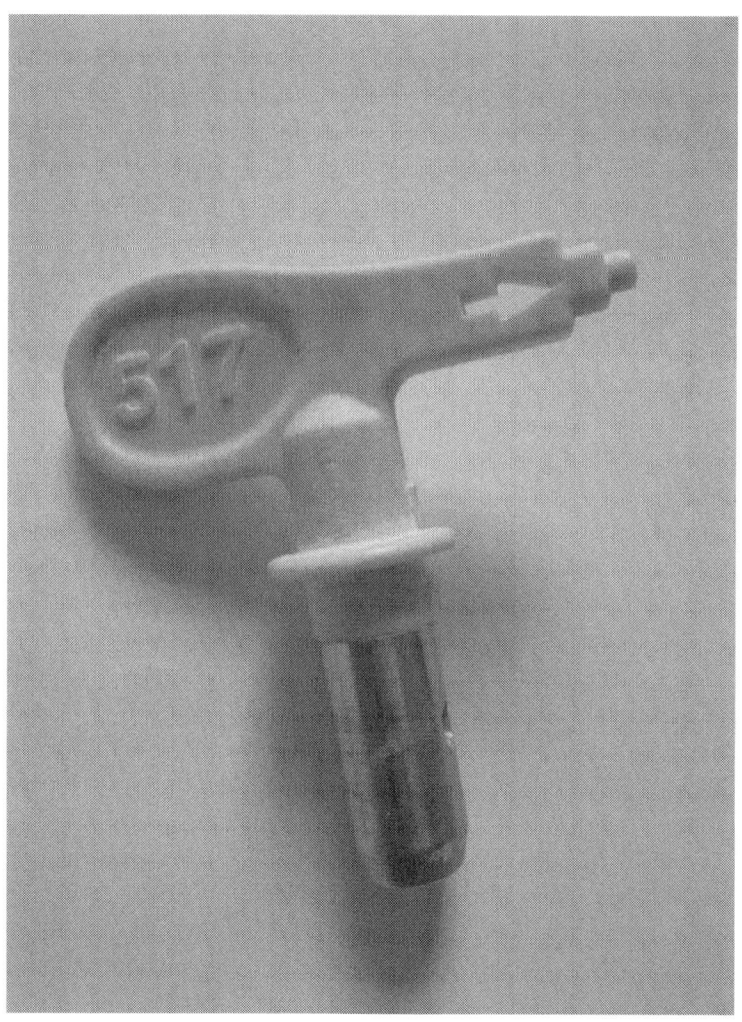

Summary; -

5 – Fan width, in this case 10" (5 x 2).

17 – Orifice size. In this case 17 thousandth of an inch.

A 517 tip is a good size for spraying emulsion.

515 – This would be good if you were spraying in a domestic house and you wanted to slow the speed of the paint down. (Smaller orifice less paint let through).

621 - would be good for spraying blockwork or new plaster. (Bigger orifice, more paint let through and a wider fan).

310 – This would be good for spraying woodwork. (Narrower fan size and slower orifice).

518 – This is a fine finish tip that is good for spraying emulsion. You have the added advantage that you get softer edges on the spray pattern and it requires less pressure to atomise the paint.

The last 2 tips are the ones that I use the most.

A note about sprayer capacity

It is worth noting here that not all sprayers can handle any size tip.

For example, Wagner; -

Prospray 3.21 airless spraypack is designed to go up to a 21 thou tip.

The larger Prospray 3.34 will drive a 34 thou tip or 2 guns at 21 thou.

You get the idea. If you have a large area to paint and you are going to use a larger tip size, then a small pump will not work.

The tip rating of an airless spraying pump gives you an excellent indication of the capacity of the sprayer and the suitability of the pump for the work that you are doing.

Paint type and tip size table

Varnishes and stain	9 – 13
Emulsion	15 - 19
Heavy duty emulsion paints	21 - 25
Block filler	25 - 35

The above is a simple table to give you an idea of how different products need a different tip size. For more information, you can either; -

1. Look at the airless sprayer manufacturers instruction booklet.
2. Get the data sheet for the product that you are using, this should have recommended tip sizes.
3. Speak to your supplier. A good supplier will have knowledge of tip sizes for various products.

Having said that you can use a 13 thou tip with emulsion if you like or even a 25 thou tip with emulsion if you want to go really fast. The above is just a guide.

Gun filter sizes

The gun filter needs to match the size of the tip that you are using.

If you are spraying with a 313 tip and you are using a white filter (see table below) then the filter may let particles through that are 17 thou. These would block the tip. Therefore, you should use a red filter which will allow particles through which are between 7 and 13 thou.

Some tips come with the correct gun filter in the same pack so that you know that you are using the right size. It can be a real pain if your gun is blocking every 5 minutes when the solution of the correct filter is a simple one.

Filter mesh sizes, colours and matching tip size.

Colour	Mesh size	Tip size		
Red	180 mesh (extra fine)	0.007"	-	0.013"
Yellow	100 mesh (fine)	0.013"	-	0.017"
White	50 mesh (medium)	0.017"	-	0.023"
Green	30 mesh (coarse)	0.023" and above		

Although the red filter is designed to work with the smaller tip sizes, I find that unless you are spraying very thin materials the red filter will clog up very quickly.

For this reason, I either use a white filter (517 tip or above) or a yellow filter (516 tip or below).

Graco filters are a different design and are different colours but the principal is exactly the same.

Chapter 6 - Using the equipment

In this chapter I want to talk about using the equipment on a job. This includes setting up the sprayer to use, using the sprayer for various tasks to get the best from the equipment and then finally cleaning up and putting it all away.

When I talk to people about spraying, they usually say something along the lines of "I cannot really be bothered to set the sprayer up I think I will just roll it. It's easier."

To a certain extent, I can understand this sentiment as for many years I have set the equipment up for the students.

Because I was only doing it once a year, I had all kinds of problems. Problems with the equipment, doing silly things and getting covered in paint or water or both. Cleaning out always seemed to be a complicated process.

When you think about it though, any task that you rarely do is a bit tricky, it's only when you do the process regularly that it becomes second nature. Now that I am spraying every day, I can set the sprayer up and clean it down in a flash and I do not see it as a hassle at all.

I rarely get equipment problems and if I do then usually these are resolved quickly.

I am going to attempt to get across a lot of the key processes but in a less dry and tedious way that many instruction manuals do. You will find that you will develop your own routine with the sprayer and vary slightly from what I am going to say.

It is also worth having a look on YouTube to see various takes on setting up and cleaning down. There is a wide range of information available on the internet, some of it questionable but some of it is very good. My favourite is "The Idaho Painter" – check it out.

Set up the equipment

It helps to think about the current state of the sprayer, there will be conditioner in the pump from the last time it was used and there will very likely to be water in the hose. First of all, attach the fluid line to the pump and the gun to the fluid line.

Make sure that you have the correct filter in the gun for the tip you are going to use. (See previous chapter for this). Plug the pump into the 110V transformer and plug the transformer into the mains.

Prepare the paint

Next you need to prepare the paint, have 2 empty 10 litre paint containers available. In one put some clean water and in another pour your paint. Depending on how much paint you are using you may want to use an empty 5 litre container.

However usually you will be spraying large amounts of paint, so you are better with a bigger container. The paint can be sprayed unthinned, however if you are mist coating plaster work for example, you will need to thin the paint up to 40%. If you are spraying a finish coat then you can still thin the paint a little so that it sprays better, maybe 10%.

Clear the conditioner out of the pump

Next place the suction hose into the paint container. Set the spray/prime valve to "Prime". We have conditioner in the pump (more on this later) so we need to clear this. To do this put the return hose in to the container of water, turn the pressure down low and switch on the pump.

This will not take long (seconds), the conditioner will be expelled into the water and then paint will start to come through. At this point switch off the pump and put the return hose into the paint container where it will stay for most of the day.

Empty the water out of the fluid line

There will be some water in the hose from last time you cleaned the hose out. The hose holds about a litre of water or paint, this is worth remembering.

Do not spray at this point or you will flood your walls with water before the paint starts to come through. Do not put the tip in the gun yet put the gun under water in the water container.

Pull the trigger, put the spray/prime valve to spray and switch on the machine.

Notice we pulled the trigger first and also put the front of the gun underwater. This is to stop the build-up of pressure from covering you with water. By pulling the trigger before switching on, the pressure does not get chance to build up. It's very likely that you will forget this a few times and get a shower at the start of the day, but you will soon get the hang of it.

Clear water will run out the hose into the bucket of water, when the paint reaches the gun, 2 things will happen. The water will start to go cloudy and the flow will change, you will notice a difference in flow from the gun because the paint is thicker than the water.

Check the spray pattern and pressure

You are now nearly ready to spray. Don't forget to insert your tip at this point. It's worth checking the spray pattern on some masking paper or scrap cardboard.

This is to ensure that all the water is gone from the hose and you are getting full paint and also to check the pressure is correct.

You should spray at the lowest pressure that gives you the correct spray pattern. You can ignore this advice and just crank the sprayer up to full pressure but if you do you will get the following problems; -

1. The tip will wear out much faster.
2. You will get lots of overspray.

3. It will put more pressure on the pump than is required.

You should turn the pressure up until you get a spray pattern with no "fingers".

Always make sure that you put the trigger lock on when you are not spraying. This is a really good habit to get into and could save your life one day.

In summary

> 1. Set up the equipment
> 2. Prepare the paint
> 3. Clear conditioner out of the pump
> 4. Empty water out of the fluid line
> 5. Check spray pattern and pressure
> 6. You are ready to spray

Typical working pressure is about 2200 psi, however this will vary depending on how thick the paint is and what size tip you are using.

Spraying

When a student sprays for the first time they usually make the same mistakes. It does not matter how long I explain the process, it does not matter how much I emphasise the pitfalls the same mistakes are made.

If after reading this, you too make the same mistakes then don't feel bad. As they say in The Matrix, "everyone falls the first time". The mistakes the students make are -

1. Pulling the trigger first and then moving the gun. This is the number one mistake that first timers

make. You need to remember that the pump can deliver 5 litres of paint (a gallon) a minute. If you hold the gun in one place for 2 seconds, then a tenth of a litre is put on the wall in one little place. Guess what? Niagara Falls, every time. To avoid this, you need to be **moving the gun while you trigger on.**

2. Not triggering off at the end of each stroke. When you get to the end of a pass you will stop the gun and move back the other way. If you do not release the trigger you will stop for a second or two in one place. Guess what? Yes, Niagara Falls. To avoid this, you need to **trigger off at the end of each stroke**.

3. Arching the gun. If you swing your hand from left to right, you will naturally form a half circle or arch. Go on try it now, I will wait.

   If you do this when pointing at a wall with a spray gun in your hand you will start away from the wall. Move close in the middle of the arch and then away again.

   This will put too much paint on the wall in the middle and too little at the edges. In fact, at the edges you will be spraying into the air causing overspray. To avoid this, you need to **keep the gun parallel to the wall.**

   This is easier said than done because it feels a little weird at first. However, if you force yourself to do this, it means moving the wrist a lot to keep the gun the same distance from the wall then you will get the knack and it will become second nature.

4. Having the gun too far away from the wall. This is not a massive problem, however it does cause overspray and wastes paint. If you waste 20% of your paint, it does not sound a lot but when you consider you could use 180 litres of paint in day you could waste 36 litres (nearly 4 x 10 litre tubs).

   Spraying too far away tends to be the beginner's choice. To avoid this, you **need to be about 12" from the wall** or a hand span (depending on how big your hands are of course but it's a good rule of thumb).

5. Having the gun too close. This is not so common, the result being too much paint on the wall causing runs. To avoid this is the same as number 4.

6. Not overlapping each stroke. This causes "banding" or stripes on the wall. To avoid this, **overlap each pass by at least 50%.** To do this aim you gun at the edge of the last stroke. Also remember that your first stroke and your last stoke needs two passes to get the coverage.

In Summary

1. Be moving while you trigger on
2. Trigger off at the end of each stroke
3. Keep the gun parallel to the wall
4. Keep the gun 12" from the wall
5. Overlap each pass by 50%

Have a go at spraying a wall and then re-read the above points. You will understand them better once you have had a go. It's not a bad idea to video yourself and then watch it back. Some of the things you will not realise that you are doing them.

Arching for example feels "right" when you are doing it because it is so natural. However, when you watch yourself doing it you will spot it straight away.

Cleaning the sprayer

Cleaning the sprayer at the end of the day is an important job. Most of the problems you will get as the sprayer gets older are due to paint not being cleaned out properly.

It's like your brushes, if you leave paint in the stock, eventually the brush is too hard to use, and you have to throw it away and buy a new one. If paint builds up in the pump of the sprayer, you will need to get the pump serviced and this will cost you money.

Cleaning the sprayer does not have to take loads of time, you will get quicker at it the more times you do it. I would allow a good half an hour at the end of the day to clean up.

To clean the sprayer, you will need a couple of buckets of warm water and an empty bucket for the dirty water. Big 15 litre buckets are ideal, but a clean 10 litre paint tub is fine.

When cleaning out the sprayer you will need to turn the pressure right down to as low as it will go. This will make the whole process much gentler.

Some sprayers have a clean setting which pulsates the water as you are cleaning. If yours has a clean setting, then this will make the process easier too.

Change the paint bucket for a water bucket

First you need to remove the paint bucket and replace it with a bucket of warm water. Not really hot or just a little bit warm, nicely warm, like you could have a shower in it. (You might do, you'll see in a minute).

Warm water will clean the pump out much better than cold, if there is no warm water on site then boil a kettle and add this to the cold from the tap.

When you remove the suction hose from the paint there will be a lot of paint around the filter area, it's worth brushing this off because it will drip everywhere as you change the bucket and it will dirty your nice clean water straight away.

Once the bucket of water is in place you are ready for the next stage.

Empty paint out if the pump and hose

At this stage there is still paint in the pump and paint in the hose. The pump does not hold that much paint, but the hose holds about a litre.

You don't want to waste this paint, if you cleaned out your sprayer every day by the end of the week you will have wasted a gallon of paint.

Firstly, put the return tube into the tub of paint that you were using. Make sure that the pump is in "prime" mode and switch on the machine. Paint will pump from the return tube into your paint bucket, it will only take a few seconds and then water will start to pump through.

Then switch the return tube into the empty bucket which is going to hold the dirty water and let the pump run a little, maybe thirty seconds.

Then switch off.

Next, we are going to empty the paint out of the hose. You need to be careful here because you do not want to spray at full pressure into a bucket as this will be very messy.

First of all, remove the tip and tip guard from the gun and put them in some water to soak.

Point the gun into the paint bucket and pull the trigger. Then change the sprayer from "prime" to "spray" and switch on. Notice that we had the trigger pulled before we switched on the sprayer. This will mean that the pressure cannot build up and the paint will be pumped into the bucket gently.

If you forget to do this, then you could end up with an unexpected shower as the gun blasts into the bucket of paint.

Don't worry you will probably only do this once.

Let the paint run until water starts to come out. This will probably take about thirty seconds. Switch the gun to the dirty water bucket and let the water run through the hose to clean it.

There will be some water in the bucket from when you were cleaning the pump, I usually put the end of the gun under water so that it does not splash everywhere. I would let this run until the clean bucket is nearly empty.

Circulate clean warm water around the system

At this stage we have circulated one clean bucket of water through the sprayer and hose.

The dirty water will be very dirty because most of the paint will be washed out at this stage. Take the dirty water and empty it, clean out the bucket and refill it with clean, warm water.

Put the suction tube into the clean water and the return tube into the empty bucket and start the process again. Switch the machine to prime and pull the trigger on the gun and then switch on (don't forget, you don't want to shower yourself) then the water will flow though the pump and the hose and you will clean both at the same time.

I keep my tips in a small plastic jar filled with tip fluid. This keeps the tips clean and stops them from drying up. Every so often I give them a blast through with water, usually when I am setting up the sprayer, just to be sure that they are clear.

Clean the pump manifold filter (if there is one)

Bigger sprayers have a filter on the body of the sprayer, next to the pump. This will have a big screw cap that can be removed, and the filter washed out.

Be sure that the pump is not under pressure when you remove this. Switching the sprayer off does not get rid of the pressure, you need to switch the sprayer to "prime" and this releases the pressure.

If the pump is under pressure the big screw cap will leave the sprayer like a bullet once loosened or you will not be able to unscrew it because the pressure will push the thread tight.

The filter and filter housing will be easy to clean at this stage because you have been circulating water through it for a while.

Once clean replace it and hand tighten the cap. Repeat the above process and circulating clean water until you are satisfied that the sprayer is clean.

Lubricate the piston with throat seal liquid (TSL)

The piston should be lubricated every day. Now would be a good stage to do it. Just a few drops of the lubrication fluid that you got with the sprayer will do the trick. Read the instructions for your sprayer to see where the lubrication point is, it is usually obvious.

Put a sticker on your pump to remind yourself to do this.

Use pump conditioner or anti-freeze

Will you be using the sprayer the next day or is it going into storage? If you are using it the next day, there is no need for conditioner.

Do not leave the sprayer in freezing conditions otherwise the water in the pump and hose will freeze and cause some damage.

If you are going to be putting the sprayer into storage, then you should use either a pump conditioner or some anti-freeze. This will help stop the internals of the sprayer from rusting and also help prevent freezing.

Follow the instructions on the bottle of pump conditioner and run it through the pump at the end of cleaning. I usually do it once I get home. That way water in the system has had chance to soak everything and when you put the pump conditioner in it will give the machine a final clean.

In summary

> 1. Change the paint bucket for water
> 2. Turn the pressure right down
> 3. Empty paint from pump and hose
> 4. Circulate clean warm water round the system
> 5. Clean pump body filter
> 6. Lubricate the piston
> 7. Pump conditioner or anti-freeze

If you want to watch a YouTube video on this process, then check out "The Idaho Painter" Search for "Cleaning an airless sprayer" or click here if this is an electronic version of the book.

https://www.youtube.com/watch?v=8p11GNYbccs4

Choosing a tip

In the last chapter we looked at tips and filters, the different sizes that are available and the correct tip and filter combination. You will find that you settle into a few tips that you use for different situations.

The most common tip size for spraying emulsion is a 517 and this works well. If I am working in a private house, I will go down a size and use a 515. This has the same fan size as the 517 but is a little slower and therefore easier to control.

If I was working on site, I would use the 517 however if you were spraying new plaster or blockwork you may move up to a 519 which would be faster.

You need to try the different sizes and see how they feel. It is surprising how much difference there is between a 515 and a 517 tip.

If you are spraying woodwork you need to use a "fine finish" tip which will give you a better finish when working with acrylic eggshell or gloss. I use either a 310 FF or a 312 FF. I prefer a 312 because it is less inclined to block and is a bit faster to work with.

Re read the chapter on tips when you have done some spraying, splash out on a range of tips, the unbranded ones are only cheap and it's good to experience the different sizes so that you really understand how they feel. You will soon be able to select the correct tip for your ability and situation.

Avoiding overspray

When I talk to people about spraying, overspray is a big topic. The general consensus is that if you spray for example the outside of a house then the whole street will get painted along with all the cars.

In the hands of an inexperienced person this could happen, so it is not complete fabrication.

If you spray correctly and take sensible precautions, then overspray should not be an issue.

There are four points to bear in mind to avoid overspray.

1. **Spray at the correct pressure**. This is generally about 2000 psi. If you crank the machine up to full pressure, then you will be blasting the paint out of the gun at a rate of knots and it will tend to go everywhere. You are not power washing your car, you only need enough pressure to atomise the paint correctly. This will vary depending on the thickness of the paint and the tip size.

2. **Do not use a worn tip.** Tips do not last forever. If a tip gets worn it will give out more paint than it's designed to do and you will get overspray, (and you will waste paint). You can tell if a tip is wearing by the spray pattern. If it is the correct size and a sharp line, then it is new.

Once it wears the spray pattern starts to go oval and then circular. You will not get correct atomisation with a worn tip. A Tip will start to wear after about 60 gallons have been put through it. I will use a new tip on every job and cost it into the price of the job. This is the most common cause of overspray.

3. **Use a shield.** A shield is basically a piece of card on the end of a pole. They can be bought from all good paint suppliers and are a useful tool to use when spraying. If you are spraying up to the end of a wall, it will be very difficult not to spray past it so a shield can be used to catch the wayward paint.

4. **Spray at the correct distance and point the gun directly at the surface.** If you arch when you spray you will get a lot of overspray. Make sure the gun points directly at the surface and that you are not too far away from the wall. Every time you spray into the air and not at the surface you are creating overspray.

In summary

1. Spray at the correct pressure
2. Do not use a worn tip
3. Use a shield
4. Spray at the correct distance and point the gun directly at the surface

Handling the hose

High pressure hoses can be a handful if they are not kept under control. The hose itself is hard and inflexible. This is so that it can withstand the pressure it is being placed under. There are a few problems that can arise with the hose and a few things that you can do to overcome them.

1. **It is difficult to turn the gun because the hose is too stiff.** The easiest solution to this is to use a whip hose. This is a short flexible hose that attaches onto the end of your normal high pressure hose. It is about 2-foot-long and flexes easily when you are spraying. You will save a lot of arm ache if you invest in one of these.

2. **Your hose is tightly coiled at the start of the job and it's difficult to uncoil**. I always loosely coil the hose when I finish the day before and hang it up. There is a temptation to coil the hose tightly around the machine so that it's out of the way. However, you will pay the price the next day trying to get the hose straight.

3. **Your hose seems to coil itself up as you work.** Every time you spray around a room you will tend to put a loop in the hose. After two or three rooms it will start to become a problem. I always uncoil the hose by twisting the gun around in the opposite direction to the loop every time I go to a new room. That way

the loops do not get chance to build up. It's a knack and it gets easier.

4. **Your hose catches the paintwork that you have just sprayed**. This is so easy to do, and the hose will cut deep lines into your lovely flawless finish.

There are three ways to avoid this.

Firstly, hold the hose in your left hand and control it so that it does not snake about.

Secondly work away from the sprayer. For example, if you are spraying a corridor you are very likely to catch the walls because it is narrow. If you pull the hose back to the sprayer and work moving away from the sprayer, then your hose will stay fairly tight as you work. Once you get to the end put the gun on the floor and go back to the sprayer and pull the gun back.

Thirdly, another method to avoid the hose catching the paintwork is asking your apprentice to hold the hose behind you and prevent it from flailing about.

This may be useful if you were in a confined space and say spraying a kitchen. For the most part if you are in a big room and you keep the loops out and hold the hose yourself you will be fine.

Spraying corners

To spray a corner, both internal and external you need to point the gun directly at the corner (at 45 degrees) and spray down it so that the band of paint goes onto both sides of the corner.

Order of working when spraying a room

One of the most common questions I am asked about spraying is "What order should I paint the parts of the room?" Traditionally when using brushes and rollers you work from the top of the room. Ceiling first and then the walls, cutting into the ceiling and then finally gloss off the woodwork last.

When spraying of course it's more difficult. If you spray your wood work last, then you have to mask the walls that you have just painted. How do you cut into your finished ceiling when spraying?

There are a number of ways that you can go about decorating a room with an airless sprayer. Maybe experiment a little with each approach and see which you prefer.

1. Ceiling last, walls first, no woodwork

    This is the standard approach that the Americans take when spraying a room. The walls are sprayed first to a finish. I have assumed the woodwork is not being done just for simplicity.

    Once the walls are finished, they are masked with low tack masking tape and plastic around the top of the wall. The plastic really needs to cover all the walls or else the ceiling paint can settle on the walls. The ceiling is then sprayed to a finish.

This approach may seem extreme but surprisingly it does not take that long to mask the walls with plastic, especially if you use a masking gun. You get a nice neat cutting in line between the walls and ceiling.

The only disadvantage is that the tape can pull the paint off the walls. If you use low tack tape and make sure you allow the walls to fully dry this will not be a problem.

2. Ceiling first, woodwork next, walls last

The next approach is to spray the ceiling first to a finish. Then spray the woodwork to a finish. I use acrylic undercoat and acrylic eggshell, satin or gloss. This gives a really nice finish and the paint does not yellow. Allow the woodwork time to harden, maybe over the weekend.

Mask the ceiling and woodwork and then spray the walls. It is quite tricky to mask the ceiling because you are upside down, but you get into it and it becomes easier.

I have used this approach when spraying walls in a room that had a new suspended ceiling and a prefinished skirting. It worked very well.

3. Ceiling first, cut in the walls. Brush the woodwork

   This is a popular approach with some contractors and works well. You spray the ceiling to a finish then once the ceiling is dry cut in with the wall colour so that there is a reasonable margin to spray to. (This depends on your skill with the gun).

   Then spray the walls side to side so that you do not catch the ceiling. Corners can be tricky because the paint can funnel up to the ceiling. Maybe use a shield. Then finally brush the woodwork.

   When I talk to decorators, they tend to think either spray everything or brush and roll everything. You can successfully mix the 2. You can spray a mist coat. This will save a lot of time.

   Then spray the ceilings to a finish. This will also save a lot of time. Then you could finish off by brush and roller if you wanted. Use the best of both worlds.

4. Ceiling first, spray the walls. Mask walls, woodwork last

   Another approach, similar to the 2 above. Finish the ceiling by spray. Then finish the walls by spray. Either cut in the ceiling or mask the ceiling, it's up to you.

Then allow the walls to dry properly and mask them around the woodwork with low tack tape and paper using the hand masker. Then finish the woodwork by spray. I have used this method very successfully.

These last two are my favourites.

5. Line the walls, spray the ceiling, and spray the woodwork. Wallpaper.

   If the customer is having all the walls wallpapered, then this is an ideal spraying job. You get a flawless finish on both the ceiling and the woodwork and there is hardly any masking because the walls are papered. Line the walls first and then spray the ceiling to a finish.

   Spray the woodwork to a finish and then finally when all the paint has dried apply the finish wallpaper.

6. All one colour

   This is quite popular at the moment, especially with student accommodation and flats. The walls and ceiling are all white and the woodwork is glossed or eggshelled.

   You can spray all the walls and ceiling to a finish very quickly because you are doing both together.

Then you can brush the final coat on the woodwork, we usually have a separate team following up behind with the woodwork while I spray the next floor.

You could spray the woodwork before the final coat goes on the walls and ceiling. When the woodwork is dry you can mask it and finish the walls and ceiling. Make sure that the woodwork is properly dry before masking.

I have tried all of these approaches with success.

The best way is to start simple and just spray the first coats on the ceiling, walls and woodwork and then finish off traditionally. Even if you only spray the acrylic undercoat on the woodwork and nothing else it will save you loads of time and give you a great finish. This will give you a feel for spraying.

Chapter 7 - Masking

"Oh, it's so time consuming."

I have a YouTube channel where I have uploaded a number of spraying videos to show my students various techniques. Check it out, search "Pete Wilkinson Decorators."

Each video has time stamp so that I know that I have sprayed a window in 30 seconds or sprayed a ceiling in 2 minutes. When I first show someone this and point out the speed of spraying the response is always the same. "Yes, but I bet it took a week to mask it all!!"

Masking is more time consuming than spraying, however it is not that time consuming. If you have never masked up a room before and you try it for the first time, then you tend to be slow and a bit useless at it.

This is because you are an amateur masker. You then make a judgement on masking based on this performance. If you watch a professional who has a lot of experience masking, then they are fast! You just need to use the right techniques and work on getting faster.

Masking is as important as spraying

Masking is a bit like cutting in. If you take care to get a good line, make sure that you cover everything then once you have sprayed and de-masked you will have a crisp job. If you rush too much with the masking and try and cut corners, then you will have a clean-up job to do after.

I can give an example of this. When masking a window there is a temptation to just mask around the edges where you are going to spray the walls and not do the centre of the window because in theory you will not be spraying there. However, it does not take much more time to mask the whole window and then there is no chance at all that you will get paint on the glass.

The customer can see that you have gone to the trouble of masking the whole window and therefore will not even look for paint on the glass.

Masking methods and materials

There are a number of products on the market for masking. It is worth exploring the market yourself and see what is out there. Try out various products and see what works for you. I will outline how I do things and what I have found works for me.

You have got 3 broad products to choose from. These are tapes, films and paper.

Masking tapes

There are a range of tapes available. I will look at them in price order.

Standard masking tape

Typically, about a £1 a roll. Available is 1" 1.5" 2" and 3" as are most tapes. Useful for basic masking, but not really great to use. I prefer it if they are supplied individually wrapped in plastic so that they don't dry up before they get used. Remove as soon as you can otherwise it will dry on and will be a nightmare to remove.

Blue painter's tape

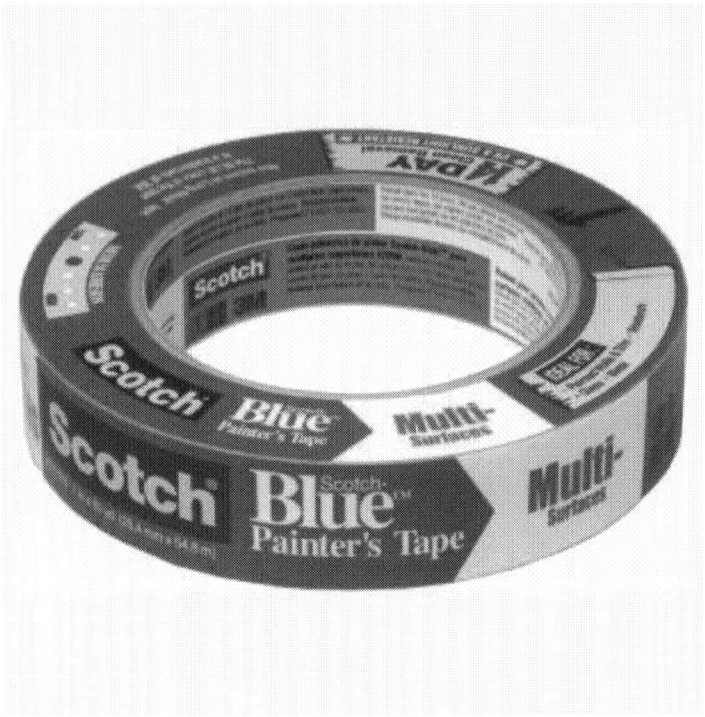

This tape is more expensive, approx. £3.50 a roll. The one shown is a 3M tape and so is the more expensive, there are cheaper brands available. I have found one that is just over £1.50 a roll.

This tape is nicer to use than the standard. You can see where you have taped clearer, it makes it easier to see that you have got a nice line. It comes off the roll better and is a little more flexible. You can leave it on the surface for up to 14 days and still remove it.

Low tack tapes

It is quite common, especially with standard masking tape for the tape to pull off the finished paint. This defeats the whole object of masking speeding up the cutting in process. To combat this there are a range of low tack tapes. The above is just one example and costs about £3.50 a roll.

Precision tape

There are a few of these on the market so do a bit of research and find one that you like. These are quite expensive, and the size shown could be a fiver. Precision tapes are for when you want a nice crisp line, for example between the lovely white skirting and the dark red wall.

Crepe tape for curves

This is about £3.50 a roll and is flexible so that is can be used for curves. It is basically crepe paper with an adhesive backing.

Edge lock tape

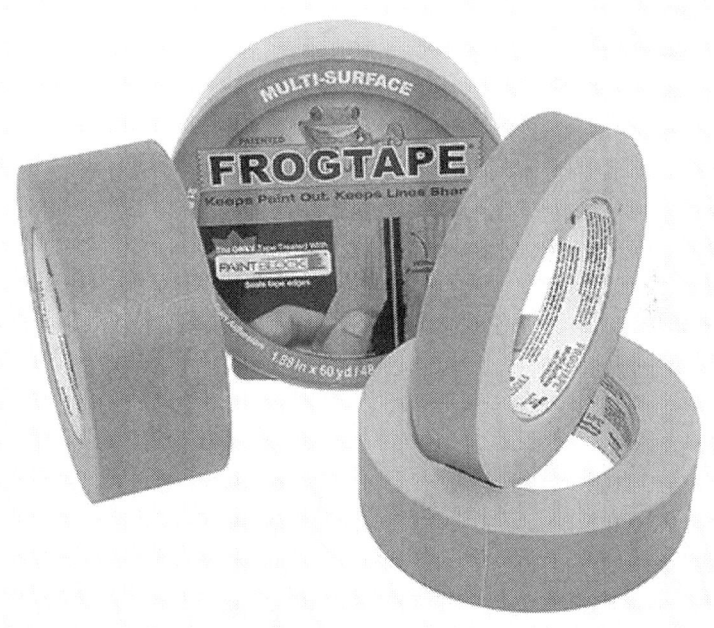

This is about £5 to £7 depending on where you go. It has an edge lock system which basically means that when the tape gets wet with paint a polymer coating on the tape expands and stops any creep. This is especially useful if you are painting with dark emulsion against a white skirting or if you are painting coloured bands on a wall as a decorative finish and the edges need to be clean. 3M also do an edge lock tape.

Masking paper

The quickest and cheapest way to mask off large areas before spraying is to use masking paper, painters tape and a masking gun. The masking machine I use is the 3M "M3000" hand masker, see below.

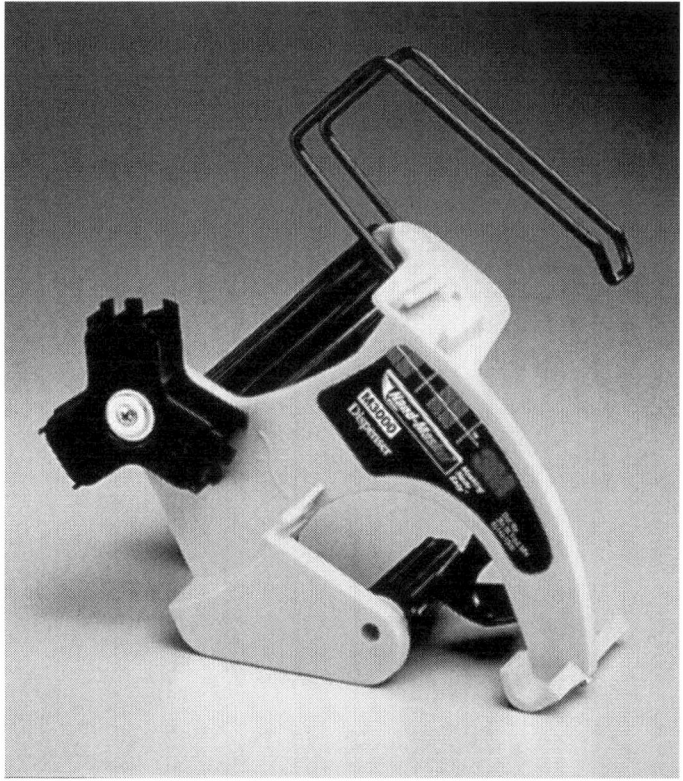

These are about £50 and are available from 3M online or Amazon.

The hand masker is essential if you are going to be doing commercial spraying work. I don't think I would use anything other than the M3000 because it is simply brilliant. It's easy to use and very robust for site work. There is a blade on the masker too which makes cutting the paper and the tape to the correct length a breeze.

The brown paper comes in various widths and is usually 50 metres long (the same as the masking tape) so that the two usually more or less run out together. A roll of paper is about £3.00 depending on where you go. I usually buy it by the box the same as masking tape.

Shown above is 30 cm wide but 15 cm wide paper is also available. I use the 30cm wide one but in some cases the narrower one could be easier to use.

Masking film

There are also clear films available to be used with the hand masker. These are great for windows and patio doors as they can be masked up for the duration of the job and they still let light into the room.

This is available in various widths and can be quite wide. Much wider than the 30cm masking paper. The above roll is 2.5 metres wide and 30 metres long, this costs about £15. However, because it is plastic it is good for protecting things like kitchen units.

Another masking film that already had the masking tape attached and therefore does not need a masking machine is tesa Easy Cover Universal.

This is available in various sizes too. This one is 2.6m X 17m and costs £9.00. I quite like these because I leave my masker loaded with paper for the woodwork etc. and use the tesa film to mask the windows.

Masking techniques

Once you have got yourself familiar with the products on the market then you need to start using these products when masking on a job. You will probably decide which products that you like the best and you will develop your own techniques for masking.

Here are some tips that I use.

Windows

On windows, I use tesa easy cover universal.

Here I have attached the tape to the top edge of the window, and it is being unravelled down to the bottom of the window.

Once fully opened out it can be masked at the side and the bottom to totally seal the window in.

Here is the window with the sides taped up.

Downlights

These are common in modern properties. The small spot lights are fitted into a hole in the ceiling.

These are amazingly easy to mask.

They are held up in the hole by 2 small springs. If you pull the downlight and gently hold the springs the whole unit will come out of the whole in the ceiling and hang free. Watch your fingers though, they are like mini mousetraps.

The best thing to do once they are hanging down is put a small freezer bag over the light and tie up.

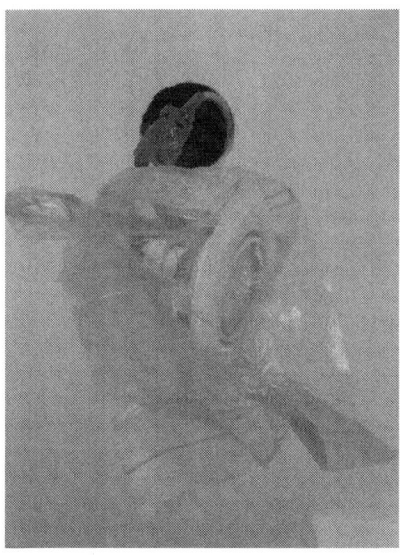

Sometimes, if the downlighters are a little tricky to drop I will mask them in situ much the same as a light switch.

Pendant light

These are also common in both domestic and commercial properties.

Pull a length of masking paper from the hand masker. Wrap this around the ceiling rose. This method is also easy to de-mask once you have finished spraying.

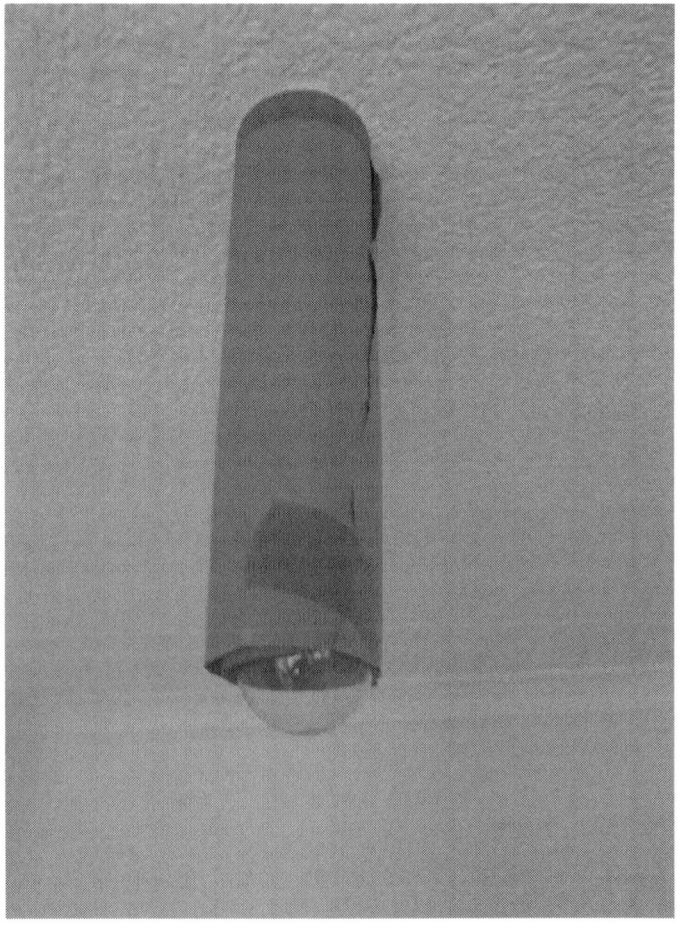

Light switches and sockets

This is one of the more common things that you will mask. Luckily, they are easy to do and you will get very quick at these. I always use inch and a half tape as this seems to work out easier when masking.

Wrap the tape around the edge of the light switch. Once it's round fold the tape onto the switch. Finally, one piece of tape should fill the middle.

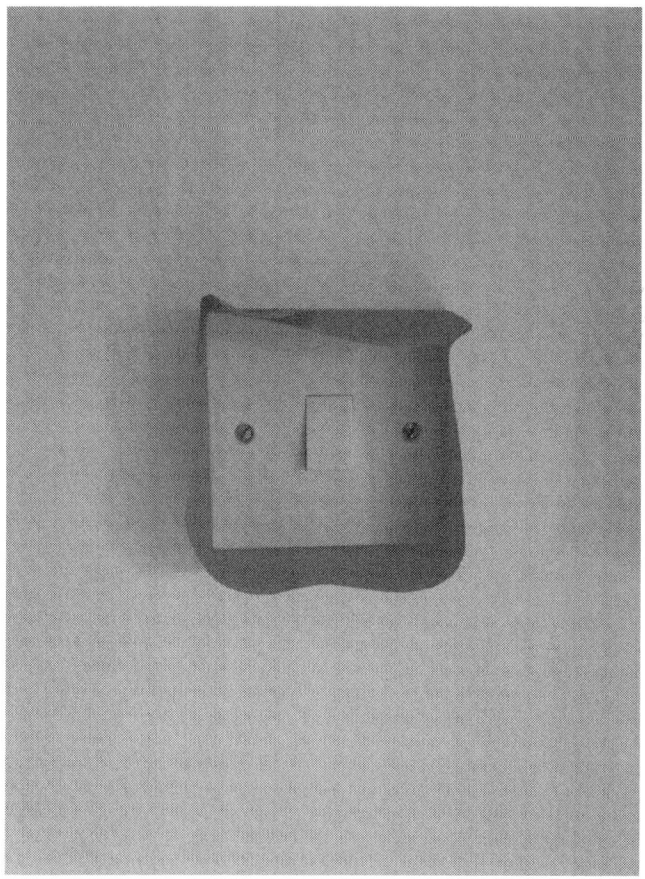

When masking sockets and light switches remember that it easier to clean a little paint off the plastic than touch up bare plaster on the wall where the tape has strayed. Because of this do not get any tape on the wall. Blue tape makes this easier because you can clearly see your line.

Smoke alarms and similar

Smaller items on the ceiling and walls are easy to mask. Pull some paper from the hand masker and wrap around in a similar way to the light pendant.

You cannot leave the tube as it is because the pressure from the spray gun will draw the paper up towards to ceiling and stick to the wet paint. You will need to roll it up and tape it so that this does not happen.

Masking glass

When masking a glass panel in a door or a Georgian window it can be very time consuming. Here is the easiest method of masking glass.

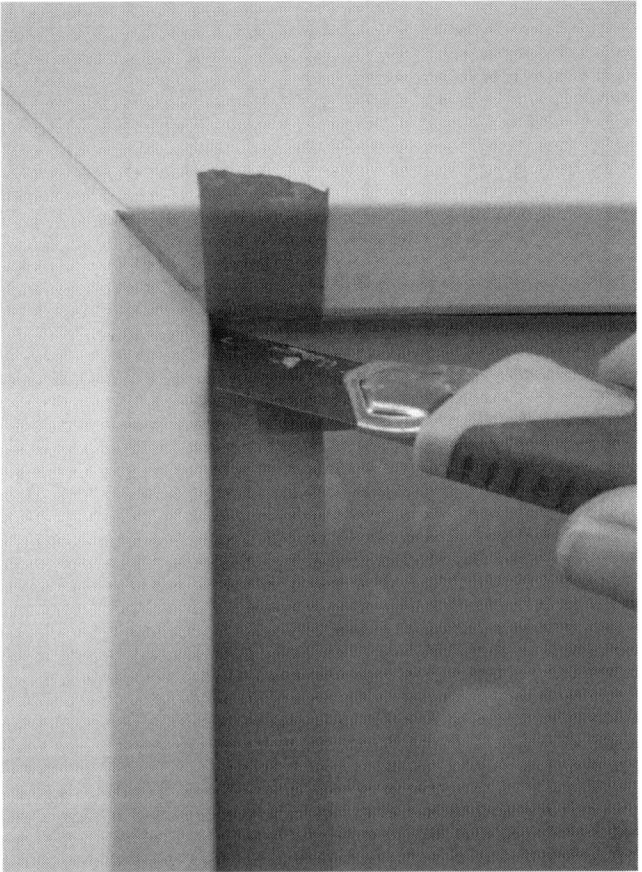

Tape the top and bottom slightly short of the edge and then tape the sides longer so that they need to be trimmed off with a knife as shown in the picture.

Here is the finished corner. You can insert paper before you tape or add the paper after and double tape the edge.

Doors and hinges

Doors are a great area to spray. It takes twenty minutes to paint one side of a door by brush and thirty seconds to spray. So it's worth spending a little time masking. The door handles are best taken off just like you would if painting by brush.

The hinges have two sides. The inside can be masked any time and the door still works ok without spoiling the masking. The outside part of the hinge is best done just before spraying.

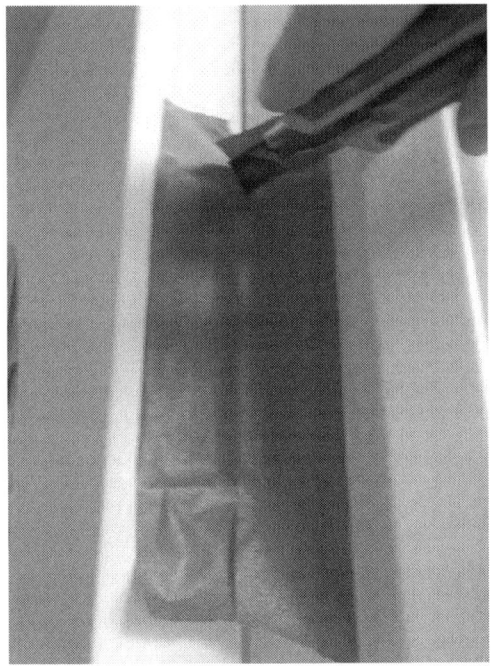

Masking the inside of the hinge. Line up the tape with the outside edge of the hinge and then trim top and bottom as shown.

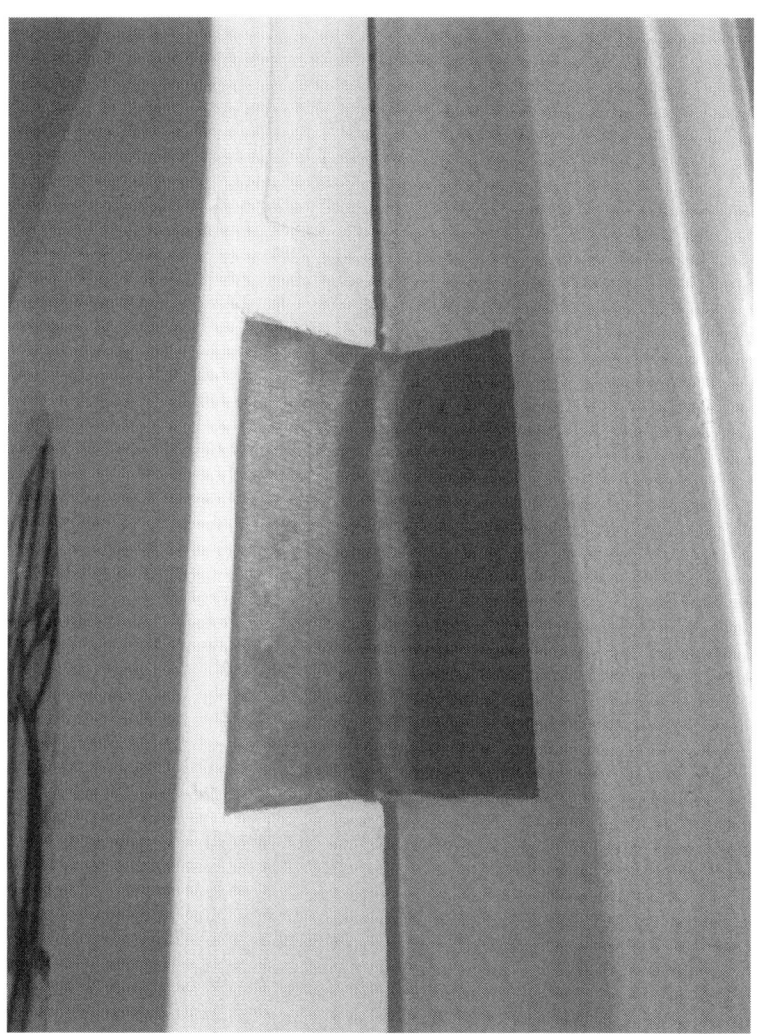
The finished hinge once trimmed.

Masking the outside of the hinge

Wrap the tape around the hinge and then pinch it closed. Do this just before spraying because it will come off when the door is opened or closed.

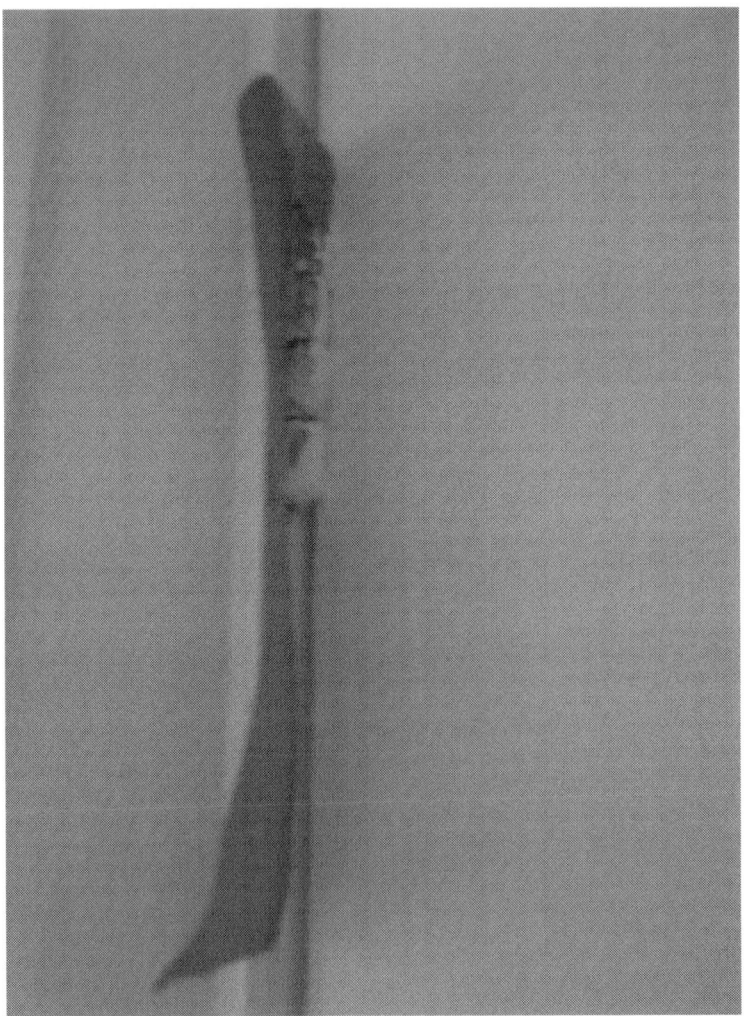

The finished hinge.

Masking skirtings

If the skirtings are prefinished or you have glossed them by spray, then you will need to mask them off. Use the hand masker to do this, it is quick and easy.

Make sure that you tack the paper to the floor with tape because the pressure of the spray gun will draw the paper up onto the walls.

Chapter 8 - Personal protective equipment (PPE) and Respiratory protective equipment (RPE)

A whole chapter on PPE! What is going on? If like me, you are a bit fed up of having health and safety rammed down your throat then you probably thinking of skipping this chapter to get onto something more interesting.

Believe me with spraying the mask is important. You cannot spray without one, if you try, I bet you don't last a full day when spraying inside. It's worth knowing about masks so that you can make an informed choice when buying one.

They are not cheap but a good one will last you. Replacement filters are available so that you can change these when needed. You'll know when.

R.P.E.

There are basically two types of mask. A particulate mask and a vapour mask. The particulate mask block particles such as dust and paint particles. The masks are graded depending how effective they are. See below.

Particulate filters

P1 – Filter out 80% of particles

P2 – 94%

P3 – 99.9%

There are a few masks on the market to say the least and it's worth looking around at various suppliers and seeing what there is. I have a couple of favourites, these are Elipse mask and of course 3M.

The Elipse masks are available at Screwfix and Amazon.

Elipse particulate mask P3

Elipse vapour mask A1P3

3M particulate

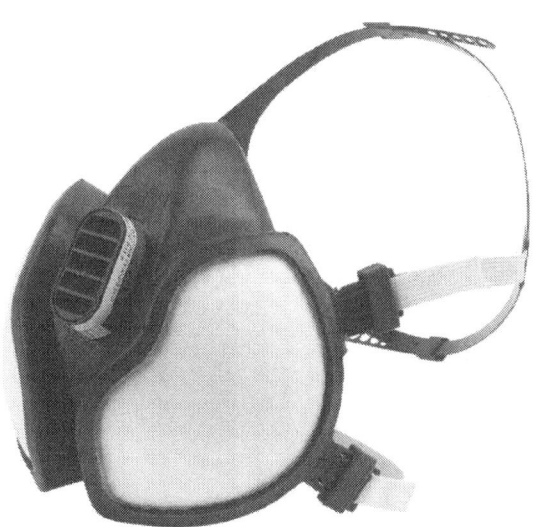

3M vapour mask

Replacement filters

I find that the Elipse A1P3 vapour mask works well both inside and outside, the mask fits well and is comfortable. It filters out all the emulsion particles. Replacement filters are fairly cheap and are easy to replace. It is important that the mask fits your face snugly otherwise particles will make their way through the gap in your mask!

Other items of PPE

Overalls

You need to wear overalls when spraying to prevent your clothes from becoming covered in paint, there are paper one piece suits that you can buy for less than a fiver. These are designed to be worn and then thrown away.

Personally, I found these to be uncomfortable and quite hot, apart from the fact you look ridiculous. However, these are cheap and worth a try to see how you feel about them. I prefer white trousers and a white T shirt. If you are spraying technique is good you will not get covered in paint and the paint that you do get on your overalls is more like a dust which washes out when you put your overalls in the washing machine.

I try and wear clean overalls every day when I am spraying but again that's not essential, I just feel that it's important to look professional and not be completely covered in paint.

Plastic glasses

If you are spraying a ceiling, you will find it very difficult not to get paint in your eyes. This can be very distracting when you are trying to spray and also, it's not good for the eyes. If you wear plastic glasses, then you can see where you are going, and you save your eyes.

These are only cheap to buy (about £3) so you can have a few pairs and throw them away when they are past their best. I just wipe them with a damp cloth after every ceiling and then I can see clearly again for the next one.

A hat

This is not essential however you will go home with white hair every night if you don't wear one. (Or whatever colour you are spraying). I wear a black woolly hat but it gets a bit hot at times. You are probably better wearing a baseball hat, I just can't bring myself to wear one. More useful if you are spraying ceilings, when you are spraying walls it's not quite as bad.

Boots and gloves

On some site's boots are required of course and you should wear them, my black boots are now white much to the amusement of the other trades. I give them a coat of black eggshell occasionally to bring them back to some kind of normality. Some painters wear gloves when using paint, I have not bothered with that, but I can see what the advantages are.

Chapter 9 – A bit about paint

One of the topics that students cover on a decorating course is "paint technology". I can hear the reader snoring already and I have not even started. I know this because typically a decorating student will ask once I start, "Why do we have to learn this?"

At first it seems like all you need to know to be a successful decorator is what products work in what situation. If you have an understanding of how products actually work and what they are made up of then you can make a more informed decision as to what paint is suitable to use.

More importantly you can explain to the customer why you are using the paint that you have chosen. Having said this, I do not think you need to know every pigment name or substances used as you can look these up.

Not that long ago decorators used to make up their own paint from their components. They would buy the basic ingredients and like a cake or a cocktail they would make up the paint to use. The modern way is to buy the paint ready-made off the shelf. The paint is made at a factory.

All paints are made from three main parts with extra ingredients added when needed. The three main components of paint are; - Medium, pigment and thinner.

The medium

If you buy a tin of varnish and open it then you are looking at a medium. There are other names for it, these include binder and film former. The medium is the main part of the paint. It is usually what the paint is named after. For example, if you are looking at a tin of polyurethane varnish then the medium is polyurethane resin. A tin of alkyd gloss is made from alkyd resin.

Mediums are made from either an oil or a resin. Oils are a natural product and traditional paints are made from this. The most common and well known oil is linseed oil. You can use raw linseed oil as a simple varnish. There are a few drawbacks, for example it will probably take a month to dry, however it will protect the wood very well and last many years.

The main advantage of an oil is that it is soft and flexible. This is essential because wood expands and contracts through the seasons and the paint must flex along with it. The main disadvantage of oil is that it is quite soft.

Along come the resins. Some natural (shellac resin and copal resin) and some man made (Alkyd, polyurethane and epoxy). Resins are hard and brittle and are ideal for situations where you need a hardwearing paint. (Floors for example). A well-known resin is polyurethane. The only drawback of resins is that they are brittle, so in our wood situation if it expands and contracts the resin can crack and the film breaks down.

So, imagine that you have set up your own paint company and you are going to produce a paint. You are faced with the following options; -

Oil - Soft and flexible.

Resin - Hard and brittle.

Which one do you choose if you are trying to make a paint that's a good all-rounder?

Well if you were really creative you would mix the two together in various ratios. This would give you the flexibility of an oil and the durability of a resin. Well it's no surprise that paint companies do this. It's called an oil modified resin.

The medium is the part of the paint that "dries", and some paints dry in a different way to others.

The pigment

I am guessing you already know what this is, it is the part of the paint that gives it the colour. Varnish of course has no pigment in it. The most common pigment is titanium dioxide or titanium white. This is what is used in white paints of course but most colours have some titanium white in them too.

A light blue for example will have a blue pigment and titanium white. It has excellent covering power or "opacity" however it is quite expensive. Cheaper paints which do not cover as well has less titanium white in them.

Approximately 4.6 million tonnes of it is used worldwide and this is increasing.

Different pigments have different opacity and light fastness. Some pigments are very poor at covering the surface. Light fastness is how well the pigment stands up to the sun. Some colours (red for example) fades quite quickly in strong sunlight.

The thinner

This is added to the paint by the manufacturer to make the paint so that it can be applied. Some mediums would be too thick to be applied by brush. You can of course add some thinner yourself before using the paint. This is not always recommended it depends on why you are thinning the paint. If you are mist coating, then it is recommended that you thin the paint by 40%. This is two litres of water for five litres of paint. Sometimes I mix it fifty fifty and it sprays fine.

The most common thinners are water for emulsions and acrylics and white spirit for oil based paints. Just as a side note the original thinner for oil paints was turpentine. This was a substance taken from the sap of trees. It was found that it was cheaper to make white spirit from crude oil. This was originally called "turps substitute" now we just call it white spirit.

Other thinners are methylated spirit used in shellac knotting and french polish. Also, cellulose thinners are used in automotive paints and some decorative paints. These two thinners evaporate very quickly and are used in quick drying paints.

Additional substances added to paint

Driers

Driers are added to oil paints to speed up their drying. You can buy driers from your paint suppliers and add it to your oil paints yourself and this will speed up the drying even more. The advantage of this of course is that the paint is touch dry sooner and there is less chance of someone touching it. The downside however is that the paint will not last as long, especially on an exterior paint job.

Extenders

Extenders are added to paint to give it more bulk or body. Pigments add bulk too but they are expensive, so cheaper powders are used to bulk out the paint more. The advantage of extenders is that they make the paint easier to apply however the disadvantage is that they have no opacity or covering power so if a paint manufacturer puts more extenders in to make a cheaper paint then it will not cover as good as one with more pigment in.

Additives

There are a number of additives that can be added to paint, these include driers, extenders, emulsifiers and biocides. Some additives are used to change the finish of the paint. For example, Satin varnish has an additive to make it satin. This additive needs to be stirred in otherwise the varnish can dry gloss.

Primers

If you are painting new surfaces, then it is important to know which primers can be used on which surface. Once the primer has been applied then the subsequent coats are the same as you would use if you were re-painting a surface. A primer is formulated to penetrate the surface in the case of porous substrates such as wood and plaster.

These primers have less pigment and more oil so that they seal the surface. A primer will have good adhesion properties for surfaces that are not porous such as glass, tiles and melamine. Here is a guide to the most common surfaces and their primers. The three most commonly painted types of surface are wood, plaster and metal.

Wood

Aluminium primer

This is used for priming wood, especially hardwood. It has sealing properties and can be used as a self-knotting primer. It is available in both oil based and spirit based paints.

White wood primer

This is used on softwoods. It is an oil based primer and is sometimes preferred to water based primer because it does not raise the grain. It is however quite slow drying and it's a good idea to leave it 36 hours before applying the next coat. (Depending on drying conditions).

Acrylic primer

This is a favourite of decorators because it can be used as a primer and an undercoat. It can be recoated in two hours which means that you could prime and undercoat easily in a day.

Metal

Zinc Phosphate

This contains a rust inhibitor and can be used on both ferrous and non-ferrous metals.

Etch primer

Used to provide a key (for better adhesion) to the metal. Used especially on metals such as zinc and aluminium.

Calcium plumbate

This contains lead and is therefore restricted. It has excellent adhesion and is the best primer for galvanised steel.

Zinc Chromate

A yellow coloured rust inhibiting primer. Can be used on ferrous and non-ferrous metals such as copper. There is talk of this being banned by 2019, so get it while you can.

Plaster

Thinned down emulsion

(Two parts water five parts paint) this is the primer for new plaster if it is going to be finished in emulsion.

Alkali resisting primer (ARP)

This is the primer for new plaster if the plaster is going to be painted in an oil based paint. The oils in the paint react to the alkali in the plaster so a special primer must be used to create a barrier and seal the plaster. The same would apply if you were painting sand and cement render.

Finishing paints

When you look at how many paints are available to finish either internal walls, external walls, woodwork and metals the choice is bewildering! To break it down a little here are the main categories of finishing paints that are available.

Emulsion

This is a water based paint used to finish internal walls and ceilings. It is not very hardwearing, but it is available in many colours and is relatively cheap. There are harder wearing versions of emulsion available such as diamond matt.

Acrylic

These paints are water based and are hardwearing. They can be used inside and outside. They are available in gloss and mid sheen finishes.

Alkyd

These are oil based paints, this is what you would be using if you were painting in an oil based gloss. It is hardwearing and is cost effective.

Polyurethane

This is a more hardwearing paint and can be used where the surface being painted is being subjected to more extreme weather or where the surface is going to get quite a lot of wear. (Floors for example).

Two pack

Two pack paints are very hardwearing and expensive. They are used in situations where the surface is going to get extreme conditions. Oil rigs, ships hulls etc. They can be used on floors and are very resistant to chemicals and wear.

A two pack paint is made from two components, a base and a hardener which are mixed together in a certain proportion. This varies depending on the type of paint and the manufacturer. 2:1 would be a typical mix with one part hardener to two parts base.

The base paint is in a tin that will fit the hardener in so that you can mix the whole tin if you like. Once mixed the paint must be used in a certain time before it goes hard. This is known as the pot life of the paint. Once hard the paint in the tin is of no use. It is best to only mix up what you actually need.

Pliolite

This is an oil based masonary paint. In this country it is probably the best one to use as it is shower proof almost immediately. Not great with the sprayer though as it would take quite a bit of white spirit to clean out.

To complicate matters further most paints, have different finishes available. For example, gloss, satin, eggshell and matt. For emulsions there is matt and silk.

Intumescent paints

These are paints that when applied to a surface will expand like foam and protect the surface for a limited time in a fire. When you compare wood and steel in a fire you would be surprised to know that steel can be more hazardous.

The reason for this is that when a thick wooden beam gets on fire it chars on the surface and this charring protects the centre of the wood for a little while. This means that you have time to get out of the building.

A steel beam when it gets hot will expand and then twist and warp, if the steel is part of the frame of the building this means the building will twist causing doors to jam closed. Intumescent paint foams on the surface of the steel will foam up and keep the heat off for a short while. (It's not magic, the building will still burn down).

These paints must be applied to a certain thickness to get a warranty, one of the best ways to apply this type of paint is by airless spray. You would need to read the manufacturer's instructions on tip size etc. as different paints vary. This type of work can be very profitable for decorators.

Preparation of paints & viscosity – ford cup & ratio stick

Most of the time when you prepare paint for spraying you will adjust the thickness of the paint or the viscosity without testing it. For example, for mist coating you will need to thin the paint by 40%. This means that you will add two litres of water to five litres of paint. The paint needs to be thinned in order for it to soak into the surface. If the viscosity of the paint is important then you can measure it.

There are two ways to do this. One is the ford cup, if you Google this you get; -

"The **Ford viscosity cup** is a simple gravity device that permits the timed flow of a known volume of liquid passing through an orifice located at the bottom. Under ideal conditions, this rate of flow would be proportional to the kinematic viscosity (expressed in stokes and centistokes) that is dependent upon the specific gravity of the draining liquid. However, the conditions in a simple flow cup are seldom ideal for making true measurements of viscosity. It is important when using a Ford Cup and when retesting liquids that the temperature of the cup and the liquid is maintained, as ambient temperature makes a significant difference to viscosity and thus flow rate.

The original Ford Cup was based on Imperial (US) measurement of the aperture"

What you do is measure how long it takes for the paint to flow through the cup into the paint container. The quicker it flows the thinner it is. Some paint manufacturers will state the viscosity that it should be sprayed at. Having said all this I have never used one myself so cannot profess to be an expert.

WFT & DFT – Combs and gauges

When a paint film dries, it gets thinner. There are two important measurements that you can make to a coating, these are WFT or Wet film thickness and DFT or dry film thickness. The wet film can be measured using a paint comb (see pictures below) and the dry film can be measured using an electronic device.

Chapter 10 – When it all goes wrong (Equipment faults)

For many years my relationship with spraying was one of anxiety.

I would be nervous when setting up the equipment because I would dread something going wrong. Especially if I had an audience. This might just be me.

More recently this feeling has gone, and I no longer expect things to go wrong and generally they don't. I think that this is one of the main reasons that many decorators don't adopt spraying as a method of paint application despite the clear advantages of speed and finish.

The excuses that decorators give are just a veneer that is covering an underlying fear that things will go wrong and there will be no way back!

Things will probably go wrong at some point, we must accept that. If you drive a second hand car, then it is likely that one day it will break down and we will call out the AA and have to get a lift to the garage.

There are a number of things you can do to minimise or even eliminate this fear.

First of all, just bear in mind that if the equipment does break down you can always brush and roll the job. If you are an experienced decorator, then you will be able to get a good finish with a brush and even though a roller is slower it's not the end of the world.

Secondly, I have a backup sprayer that I can use if the main machine does break, this is comforting to know. I have not had to use it yet. If you do not have a second sprayer you could hire one in an emergency if you had to.

Thirdly, keep your machine well maintained. Clean it thoroughly, use throat seal every day to keep the piston lubricated. Take the sprayer for a service every year or couple of years. This will all but eliminate problems.

You will see painters using old machines that have never been serviced, cleaned properly or serviced and then when they break down there is surprise on their faces.

Many contractors use their company's equipment which is not really looked after as well as if you had your own sprayer. Many contractors fall into lazy habits such as leaving the paint in the machine all week and only cleaning it out at the end of the job. That's your choice but it's not a good habit to have.

The following are common equipment faults which I have experienced along the way; -

Ball bearing stuck

This can be a common problem with piston pump airless sprayers. There is a ball valve on the suction tube which allows paint to be drawn up from the paint bucket but does not let it back out again. When you wash out the sprayer and then come to use it again the following week the ball can get stuck.

When you try and prime the sprayer it just runs and runs and does not draw up any paint. The piston can get quite hot so be careful that you do not run the machine for too long without seeing paint coming back out of the return tube.

There are a number of remedies for this. I have an old Wagner EP2300 at college and the ball always sticks, I am not sure if it is because it's old or if it is just the model of machine. Before I use it I always screw the suction tube off and free the ball bearing valve with my finger. It's easy to do when it's clean but difficult when it's all full of paint. I do this every time so that I know that it is free.

I have a brand new Wagner machine that has a little plunger on the outside of the machine that you can press at any time and it frees the ball bearing. This is a handy little addition to the modern sprayers, I have not had need to use it yet, but I am sure that as the machine gets more use the ball bearing will stick.

I was using an old Graco 495 sprayer on a big contract that we were starting. It was the first day and I set the machine up. Put the suction tube into the paint and switched it on. Nothing. The piston started to get warm, still nothing. A gentle clout on the piston housing near where the ball bearing valve is with a spanner freed the ball and the paint started to flow. Sighs of relief all round I can tell you.

Once you get to know your machine you will know how often this happens, if it happens at all and what you need to do to free it.

Tails in your spray pattern

When you start to spray you should do a test band on the wall or a piece of card to make sure that your pattern is nice and solid. If you get "tails" or "fingers" which basically means the pattern is not a solid block, then you are probably spraying with the pressure too low. You can remedy this by slowly turning the pressure up until the test pattern is solid.

You may find that you have turned up the pressure to full and the spray pattern still has tails. This could be that the paint is too thick for the size of sprayer you have. A smaller sprayer will struggle to atomise thicker paints, even on full pressure.

To remedy this, you will need to thin the paint until you get a solid pattern. If you are in a situation where you cannot thin the paint because of the specification of the paint, then you may have to hire a larger machine that can handle the paint.

Another reason for tails may be a blocked filter in the gun or too small a filter in the gun. This can prevent enough pressure from reaching the gun and therefore not being able to atomise the paint properly. To remedy this check that you are using the right filter and check that it is not blocked.

No paint at all when you pull the trigger

This has happened to me a few times when doing a demonstration in class. I will let the students clean out the sprayer and put things back together and this is not always done correctly.

If the pump has primed successfully but when you switch to spray and pull the trigger nothing happens then this points to a blockage somewhere along the line.

The tip could be blocked either because it was not cleaned out properly last time or because the paint has bits in it and it has not been strained. Try a new tip to eliminate this problem. I always have a brand new tip in my box so you can try this with confidence.

Look at the filter in the gun. I had one instance where the filter has not been washed out at all and was just caked in dry paint. This would prevent any paint passing through the gun to the tip. Change the filter for a new one. Filters are cheap and there is no reason to be working with one that is blocked.

This next filter problem had me foxed for a while one day when the gun would not work. The pencil filter had been put back in the gun the wrong way around when the last student had cleaned it out. There is only a hole in one end of the filter so putting it in the wrong way around effectively blocks the gun. Simple once you know but drove me round the bend trying to find it. Some pencil filters are screw in so that this cannot happen and Graco filters are open both ends so it cannot happen with those either.

If your sprayer has a manifold filter, then it is worth checking to see if this is blocked. I have spoken to one or two painters that did not even realise their machine had a manifold filter let alone clean it out every time. If this is blocked, then clean it out or change for a new one.

You are starting to run out of options to look for now. The hose could be blocked, unlikely if it was cleaned correctly the last time it was used but possible. Try another hose to eliminate this possibility. There could be a faulty pump/prime valve. I would maybe be thinking about getting the spare sprayer out at this point.

Spitting

Extension poles are great, you can buy then in various sizes, they are fairly cheap and the allow you to reach ceilings without using steps and spray walls without bending and stretching. They do however spit when you trigger off. Because your trigger stops the paint flow at the gun but does not stop the paint still in the pole. There are a couple of remedies to this.

If you are spraying a ceiling with an extension pole, then you can spray backwards and forwards without triggering off in one continuous motion. You need to be very quick when you change direction because for a split second when you change direction the gun is stopped and if this lasts more than a fraction of a second then you will get build up at the edges of the ceiling. I however do this with no problems.

Another solution is the Graco clean shot valve which can be attached directly to any extension pole and will prevent spitting by cutting off the flow of paint at the very tip. These are quite expensive but probably worth the investment if you do a lot of spraying using extension poles.

Tip blockage

If your tip blocks when your spraying it can really interrupt your flow. Tips are reversible which means that if a particle that is too big to go through the orifice size that you are using sticks in the tip then you can trigger off, reverse the tip and blow out the particle into a suitable place.

If this only happens once when you are spraying, then it's not too bad but if it's happening every two minutes it can get annoying. If this is the case, then you can check a few things out.

Firstly, if your filter is bigger than your tip then it will let particles through that the tip cannot handle. For example, if you are spraying with a 310 tip, this has an orifice size of ten thou.

If you are using a fifty mesh filter then this will allow particles through that are up to seventeen thou, obviously the tips going to block a lot. Change your filter to the correct size for your tip.

Secondly it is possible that your filter has a tear in it and is therefore not filtering properly and letting larger particles through to the tip. To remedy this, take your filter out, wash it and check for rips or tears. If it is faulty then put a new filter in. I would put a new filter in anyway just to eliminate this possibility.

Finally, there may be no filter in the gun at all. Before you comment on who would do this, all I can say is I wouldn't be surprised! It's amazing what habits people get into.

Not priming or no pressure

With a piston pump, the pressure is created using a piston in a cylinder. There are rubber seals that keeps the pressure from escaping and this is what pumps the paint. This part of the sprayer will wear out in time and need replacing.

If your sprayer is losing pressure or not priming and you have been using the sprayer a while since new or its last service, then it is likely that the pistons or seals or both need replacing.

One of the things that prolong the life of your seals and pistons is regular lubrication with throat seal liquid (not oil) it is recommended that you do this every four hours of continuous use.

I have spoken to a few decorators that use airless sprayers and asked them how often they use throat seal liquid and so far, I have gotten a blank look back. If you don't do this your seals and pistons will not last as long.

If you are not getting pressure, then you can take your sprayer for a service. If you are lucky and you only need new seals then this will not be too expensive, however if you need a new piston too then it will be.

You can buy kits from the manufacturer and do this yourself, it's not that difficult and if you own a few sprayers and do a lot of this kind of work it would be worth getting your head around. However, if not it's probably worth getting the machine serviced. Usually the place that you bought the sprayer from will organise this for you.

Kinks in the high pressure hose

High pressure hoses are quite expensive, so they are worth looking after. Coil them up carefully after use and hang them up.

When you are using the hose make sure it is uncoiled and free to use. If you pull and tug on the hose when spraying this can cause a loop to kink and this could then split and leak paint (at 2000 psi it's not like a leaky water hose).

If the hose does split it must be replaced, do not be tempted to fix it with a jubilee clip or similar, this is dangerous and just not worth it.

Chapter 11 – Spraying in the real world

In this chapter I am going to relate some stories from real jobs to illustrate how common misconceptions are not the case and to show that you can produce excellent work using an airless sprayer.

I regularly talk to other decorators about spraying and find that they fall roughly into three camps. First is the "I don't do that kind of work and never have." These guys are usually paperhangers who do mainly domestic decorating work.

The second camp is the "I am sold, and I use a sprayer on jobs whenever I can." These decorators have gone down the spraying road and have found it to be profitable. These decorators are on the same page as me and we swap stories of spraying jobs gone by.

The final camp is a little on the fence. They have thought about spraying, maybe even done a bit working for a firm but they are sceptical. They have a number of well thought out objections, some of which are valid, and some are myths.

The following are some of the myths.

It would be quicker to roll

This is a popular one. Why bother with all the fuss it's quicker to roll anyway? It isn't quicker to roll, let's not kid ourselves. I wish it was quicker to roll but it isn't, it's about four times quicker to spray. Granted if you are emulsioning one ceiling in a lounge then it *could be* quicker to roll but even then, I doubt it.

If you are painting 10,000m2 of new plaster believe me it's quicker to spray. We had a contract to spray some apartments, there were fifty of them. They were being stripped out, no carpet or furniture. The ceiling was white and the walls where white. We sprayed these and we were doing a floor a day, fifteen rooms, three corridors and three kitchens. The added bonus was that the effort required was less than with a roller.

Masking is slow

When you spray a room, you will need to mask anything that is not being painted. Much like you do when you roll. The carpet needs to be covered, the sockets need to be masked, and so do the windows. When I first started masking, I was slow, after a bit of practice just like with painting you get quick at it. Once you resist the urge to paint straight away and just get on with the masking it does not take long.

We did a job in Leeds which was quite a big area of walls to be emulsioned. The ceiling was a brand new suspended ceiling and there was quite a bit of masking. I think to roll the area we were painting would have taken three or four days. It took us until three in the afternoon to mask however once I started spraying the whole lot was first coated in three hours. The next day took three hours to second coat and the masking was removed in no time.

Another example of the time saved with masking was a hallway landing and stairs that I did recently. There was a lot of doors, skirting and of course spindles and the staircase. It would have taken at least a day to paint by brush. That would be three days if you gave the woodwork three coats.

The masking took two hours. The walls were finished, I was only doing the woodwork. I then sprayed the lot in thirty minutes. It would be then possible to put on three coats in an hour and a half. Once de-masked the "cutting in" was perfect, as was the satin finish.

Three coats was done in half a day. This is six times faster than using a brush, even with the masking and the finish was amazing.

Masking materials are expensive and it's quicker to cut in

This is another popular one, it's quicker to cut in. Unfortunately, again it's not. I can mask a line quicker than I can cut in a line and I am very quick at cutting in. That's just with one coat. If you are spraying a window and you are giving it three coats, then once its masked there is no "cutting in" on the remaining coats.

I did an outside job which involved painting ten sash windows. Normally of course these would be brushed, each window would be cut in. A window would probably take twenty to thirty minutes a coat. Three coats with rubbing down probably two hours a window. Ten windows is twenty hours. This is just under three days.

I decided I was going to spray them. It took three hours to mask them, however once masked it took thirty seconds to apply a coat of paint. I applied three coats of paint in about thirty minutes (obviously there was drying time in between) the finish was flawless, the customer could not believe it.

Imagine if there had been a hundred windows.

The sprayer uses a lot more paint than a roller or brush

Spraying does use more material than a brush or roller. However, it does not use that much more, and you can control this. I like the fact that spraying puts a good coat on. In a lot of circumstances this is actually an advantage. We did a job where it was split into two parts. Another contractor was doing one part using brushes and rollers and we were doing our part by spray.

The walls were magnolia and they were being finished in white emulsion. The firm rolling could not make the walls cover in two coats and therefore had to bill the customer for three coats. We easily made the walls cover in two coats using the sprayer. I use it as a selling point, the sprayer gives you two coats in one. If you move the gun quicker, it will put less on the surface and it will use less paint. If you use a smaller tip then this will also use less paint.

A common problem with airless systems is that the tips do not last as long as contractors would like them to. A new tip will be very efficient with the paint. Once the tip wears then it will start giving you a narrower spray pattern and start using more paint.

A tip will vary with how long it lasts however a rough guide of about sixty gallons per tip. Check the spray pattern after this time. There should be a crisp line and the fan width should match the tip number. For example, a 517 tip should have a 10" fan pattern. If it has an 8" pattern and is starting to look round, then the tip is worn.

A worn tip will use much more paint, because the fan width is narrower you need more passes to cover the wall. A worn tip could cost you the price of a new tip every day in wasted paint easily.

You get loads of overspray, everything will get covered in paint

Overspray, this is stated as a reason not to spray so many jobs. Ok you do get overspray and you do have to mask up and sheet up in an area where you are spraying. If your technique is good and your tip is not worn, then you will not get that much overspray. If you arch the gun and you are spraying into the air, then this will create lots of overspray.

If you are spraying to the edge of something without a shield, then you will get overspray as the spray goes past the edge of the wall that you are spraying. In the hands of a competent sprayer you could spray the outside of the garage with your van on the drive and you would not get any overspray on the van.

Don't believe me? Then check out - "Controlling paint overspray" just do a search on YouTube.

You can't touch up the finished product

This is another common fear that decorators have. In fairness if you are spraying new plaster then you do get a flawless finish, no roller marks or brush marks. This is good surely. Just because we have always painted using methods that give a poor finish does not mean that we should continue to work this way.

There was a time when people wanted a brush finish and did not like the orange peel effect of a roller. Oh, how we have moved on! I can see the point though, in some firms the finishing team and the touch up team are different. The touch up guys do not spray so this could be a problem.

There are a number of solutions. Firstly, bear in mind that if you are redecorating and the previous coats are rolled (likely) then this will still show through the sprayed finish (unless you sand the orange peel out) This means that you could still touch up with a mini roller and it would not show.

Another approach is to spray the first coats on the walls and ceiling. Spray the final coat on the ceiling but roll the final coat on the walls. This would not be my first choice, but a lot of companies do this. You save time on the first coats, but you are still able to touch up easily.

Some companies back roll the spray finish on the final sprayed coat. This gives you the speed of spraying on the final coat but puts a roller texture in the finish coat so that it can be touched up.

Finally, Graco make a cordless handheld airless sprayer for touching up. I have not used this method myself however with matt emulsion this should work fine.

Sprayers are very expensive

Any company that wants to make more money by improving their processes will have to invest money in either training their workforce with new methods or new equipment that will speed things up, or most likely both.

Let's have a look at some costings to see if it is worth buying a sprayer. I will assume a fairly low figure of £20,000 worth of decorating work in a year. Also, we will assume that you only use the sprayer on half of your work, so that's £10,000.

The sprayer is four times faster so you will get the £10,000 worth of work done in a quarter of the time, this means you can do more work or have lots of holidays. If you do more work, then that's an extra £30,000 worth of work. A typical sprayer costs £1,000 so you are left with £29,000 extra money.

Ok, let's be a little pessimistic about our figures. Let's say you will only use the sprayer on ten percent of your work and it's only twice as fast. So, ten percent of £20,000 would be £2,000 and you would do it twice as fast and have time to do another £2,000 worth of work. Sprayer paid for again, easily.

In reality and in my experience the first situation is more common, and you will find that your earnings with triple or quadruple when you start spraying. It's difficult to believe I know. This will not happen overnight, it may take twelve months to build up to that.

Sprayers keep breaking down and are costly to repair

More or less everyone I know drives a car. These are expensive things to have. They are a few grand to buy. Then you have insurance, car tax, MOT, servicing and if it breaks down, expensive garage fees. If you look after your car it is less likely to break down. You would never go back to having a horse and cart though. I don't know anybody who has done this.

It's the same with a sprayer except they are a lot cheaper than a car to buy. You don't need tax, insurance or and

MOT. Yes, it will need a service every couple of years, but this will be cheaper than a car service.

Worst case scenario, the sprayer breaks down, you get out your brushes and rollers and away you go. It's not the end of the world. I guarantee though that you will get your sprayer fixed, going back to rollers is like when you come off the motorway after doing seventy and thirty miles an hour feels like you are going walking pace.

You cannot spray woodwork or smaller items

I have spoken to quite a few decorators who have some experience of airless spraying telling me that you cannot spray woodwork. I spray woodwork all the time.

Oil based glosses and eggshells go yellow very quickly due to the new VOC regulations, so you have to use acrylics on domestic work and commercial. The only disadvantage of acrylics is that they are harder to get a good finish with a brush.

This is not the case when you spray the woodwork. You will get a mirror like finish when you spray acrylic gloss or satin. For me there is no other way.

They are dangerous to use

Airless is dangerous I am told. The 2000 psi pressure can cause *fluid injection*. Well yes, if you are very careless. If you lie in front of a bus when it sets off, you will get killed too.

Respect the machine and there is no problem. Google this but don't let it put you off.

Chapter 12 – Pricing for profit

One of the things that I have realised while I have been doing the spraying courses is that pricing correctly and spraying go hand in hand. Before I start preaching to you about pricing, I want you to know that I am by no means an expert. If you take on board what I am about to say and decide to change the way you price then I recommend that you find a good freelance estimator or quantity surveyor who can sit down with you, look at your business and help you develop your own set of "rates".

While I am teaching decorators how to spray, I always take a minute to talk about how they price. Most of the people I speak to will price by estimating how long the work will take, then they multiply that by their "day rate" and finally add an estimated cost for materials.

Before we go any further discussing pricing let's pause for a minute to consider "day rate". I am quite frequently asked by my customers "What is your day rate?" This is a question that I will not answer unless they are one of my decorator friends that I work for.

Just consider the following set of day rates.

Andy   £80 per day

Bob   £120 per day

Clint   £150 per day

My question to you would be – **"Who is the cheapest?"**

Just ponder for a minute before you turn the page…..

Most people who I have asked this question would answer that Andy is the cheapest because he is only charging £80 per day. However now consider some additional information. Each decorator has completed the same job and here is how it panned out. Bear with me it's only a story and we are pretending that the customer has supplied the paint. Never do that either by the way.

Andy (He is a third year apprentice) £80 per day
Job took 4 days **Total cost £320**

Bob (Been decorating 5 years) £120 per day
Job took 3 days **Total cost £360**

Clint (Very productive) £150 per day
Job took 2 days **Total cost £300**

With this additional information you can now see that Clint is actually the cheapest decorator out of the 3 candidates. I am not suggesting it's good to be the cheapest (it's not) I am suggesting that you cannot tell how cheap someone is by their quoted day rate. Many customers will ask you this question and the only reason they are asking is to try and judge how expensive you are.

Ok Pete we are with you so far but big deal, what is your point? Well the point is that now you have read this book you are about to become a lot more productive. That job that used to take you two weeks is now going to take four days. If you stick with your day rate approach you are actually going to be turning out more work but still only getting the same money.

When we learn how to be a decorator, we generally do this at a firm, we learn all of our practical skills while we are protected from all the business side of things, someone else does that. Once we decide to work for ourselves, we can easily forget that pricing is a skill like any other that has to be learned and practiced. In fact, it is the most important skill that you will learn because it does not matter how good you are at your trade if you cannot price correctly you will struggle to make a good living.

You did not leave your firm to make less money and have less freedom, you left so that you had full control of your time and you were going to make more money. To do this you will need to price correctly.

We have just left our firm and set up on our own. I have two questions for you.

1. What type of work are you likely to be doing?
2. How will you price it?

The answer to the first question is most likely that you will be doing small (under £1000) domestic jobs. The answer to the second question is that to price it you will probably guess.

Hang on a minute.

Guess??

Yes, that's right you will guess how long the job will take based on your experience and you will multiply that guess by a day rate that you have been told is the "going rate". Ok in fairness we are pretty good at guessing, especially if we have done a lot of domestic type work.

Bear in mind though it is human nature to under estimate the time it takes to do a task.

This method will work reasonably well on small jobs if it's just you who is working on them. Once you have been in business for a while you will get busy and you may decide to take someone on who can help you.

Now there are two of you. Let us call the new guy Dave. You price a job, you guess it would take you five days. Dave starts the job and surprise surprise Dave does not work as hard as you and the job takes six days. You lose money.

You have a word with Dave and on the next job you set him a target, "This job will take you five days Dave" you say. Dave rushes the job, bumps it and gets it done in five days. The customer is not happy though and you have to go back and spend a couple of days putting it right.

You begin to realise that your guessing only works with you and when you are guessing for Dave you have to have a different set of times. This starts to lead to inconsistent prices and people only wanting you on their decorating because you are cheaper and better.

Another reason why guessing starts to break down in time is that it does not work with bigger jobs. You can fairly accurately guess how long it takes to emulsion an average size lounge but what about a 300 bedroom hotel? Any errors on a 5 day job are going to be small but an error on a big job could cost you a lot of money.

Let's pause a minute to think about how prices are actually set in a real market place. In reality there is a market price for anything. Let us look at a house as something that has its price set by the market. There are so many people selling houses and so many people wanting to buy houses.

If there are more people wanting houses than there are for sale, then the price is forced up. If there are more houses for sale that people need then the price will fall or go stagnant for a while (which is actually falling due to inflation).

Ok let us look at another example that's more like what we do. Carpet fitters. These guys charge by the square metre. For example, £6 per square metre. This rate is set by how many carpet fitters there are and also how many people want their carpet fitting.

If there are more people wanting carpets fitting than there are fitters to do the job, then the rate will go up to maybe £7 per metre. If there is a fall in demand, then the rate may fall to £5 a square metre.

If I want my front room carpeting then I measure the room, it's 300 square metres (oh no drifted off there thinking I owned a mansion) it's more like 20 square metres. So, the price to carpet my lounge (labour only) is £120.

If you said to the carpet fitter "How long do you think it will take you?" he will have a blank look, scratch his head and wonder why you want to know that. All fitters charge by square metre what difference does it make how long I take?

The good thing for the carpet fitter is that if he is very good at his job and can fit carpets fast and do a good job (a fast and flawless carpet fitter) then they will be well rewarded and so they should be too.

I think you are getting the swing of it now. We are aware of rates as decorators because this is how commercial work is priced. Domestic work we are told cannot be priced this way. I think this is wrong, we can price using rates on any type of work.

But what if the walls are in a poor state of repair and need more work to get them right, well then use a higher rate for that kind of work.

So, let's look at a decorating example that we can start to use. The typical rate to apply emulsion to walls (2 coats plus prep) is anywhere between £4 and £10 per square metre. It depends on where you live and your reputation (and therefore how busy you are).

Now when you price a job it becomes so much easier. You measure up how many metres the walls are. A typical lounge will be about 40 square metres. This would give us a price of £160 on the lower £4 a metre rate. This price would be the same if you are doing it or our new employee "Dave" is doing it.

After working with your rates for a while you can look at how long jobs are taking to complete and check if you are making the profit that you want to make. If you're not, then you need to raise the rate. If you are really busy and demand is outstripping supply, then you need to raise your rates. Finally, if work is slowing down a little you can lower your rate to win more work.

"I hate maths though, I was never good at it"

I have news for you, **everyone** hates maths and think they are not good at it. I have taught thousands of students at college, apprentices, adults and full time students and no-one feels confident with maths. The good news is that the maths that you need is very straight forward and repetitive and you can get equipment to help.

I am not going to get bogged down with the ins and outs of working out the area of a wall because I know that if you google it or go on YouTube there will be a simple tutorial which will teach you. It's worth the effort.

I am not going to give you a set of rates either because you need to develop your own, which match your geographical location and your position in the market. You can buy a "SPONS" book which will give you a set of rates, but the book is quite expensive (look on Amazon) and it's a bit mind blowing. You are better to find someone who estimates for a living and spend a day with them.

To make measuring easier I use a laser tape measure that I bought off amazon for just over £20 and you place this against one wall and a laser bounces off the other wall and back and the device gives you a measurement. Great for measuring high ceilings or long corridors.

One final tip for people making the change to a new way of pricing. First of all, guess and write down how much you would "normally" charge. Then measure up, price with your rates and see how it compares. If you would normally charge £1000 for a job and the price with rates comes out at £10,000 then I am guessing that you pressed a button wrong on your calculator.

It's up to you if you want to include materials in your rate. Materials can vary very widely in price depending on the quality of the product, so you may decide to add the material cost on top of your basic labour rate. However, if you always use the same standard product's then you may want to build that into your rate.

Here is how you would work out a material rate.

Let's assume that 10 litres of white emulsion is £30. This is just an example for the book, I am sure that you pay less. How far will that paint go?

Well typically it will cover 12 square metres per litre. 10 litres will cover 120 square metres.

£30 of material will do 120 square metres.

£30 divided by 120 is 0.25

That's 25 pence.

We now know that if we have some walls that are 40 square metres and it is being painted in white emulsion it will cost us £10 in material. (40 times 25 pence).

You can see that the labour cost for this was £160 and the material cost is £10 so that material cost is quite small compare to the labour in this example. Coloured emulsions would be more of course. Let us do one more example with coloured emulsions on the walls.

Let's assume a price of £45 for 5 litres of coloured emulsion.

5 litres will do 12 metres a litre times 5 = 60 square metres (half the ten litre tub obviously so it only goes half as far).

£45 divided by 60 metres (how far the paint goes) = 0.75 per metre.

75 pence a metre.

It more expensive because the emulsion was quite a bit more expensive and it came in a smaller tin than last time.

Your walls now cost 40 square metres times 75 pence = £30 for materials.

So, labour is £160, and materials is £30. This is actually quite typical, my old boss used to say that material cost is normally 20% of the job. If it's a £1000 job, then materials will be £200. I know it depends on a lot of things but it's a great rule of thumb.

You would need to do similar calculation for the different products that you use so that you know how much they are costing you per metre. It even works with wallpaper, but you usually know that cost of that beforehand anyway.

You could combine the labour and material costs together and have a rate of £4.75 per metre but I personally think it's easier to manage them separately. It's up to you, you're the boss these days.

Some things like filler, sandpaper and white spirit you can add as a sundry item to the job. So just add £50 (as an example) for bits and bobs, depending on the size of the job of course.

I hope this has given you some food for thought, and I hope you didn't skip this chapter because you hate maths, you are never going to get that BMW M3 or a luxury holiday for the family if you don't know how to price properly.

Chapter 13 - Common paint defects

It is important to be aware of what can go wrong with the application and use of paint. I have tried to keep it brief and informative. There is the name of the defect, what it actually is and how it occurs and finally what to do about it if you come across the defect or create the defect yourself.

I must confess that I have created some of these defects inadvertently in the past myself. Unfortunately, we sometimes learn best from our mistakes, however if you are new to decorating or spraying then here is a chance to shortcut learning the hard way.

This is not a completely exhaustive list. I did not want to create a dictionary of paint defects. I have selected what I think to be the most likely defects that you will come across, plus a couple with long names so that you can impress your friends at parties. The defects are in alphabetical order.

Banding

What is it?

Banding is where the paint appears on the surface in stripes where some of the surface has been missed by the paint.

Solution

When spraying a surface, it is important to overlap each stroke by fifty percent so that after two passes the surface has had a double coat. This avoids banding occurring.

Bittiness

What is it?

Bits and nibs in the paint coating caused by using paint which has not been strained or a dusty environment. Although less likely when spray applying paint, this can still happen. Especially if there is dust or dirt on the floor or on the top of door casings. The pressure from the gun will blow the dirt onto the painted surface.

Solution

Strain the paint before use. Make sure the area is swept and mopped before painting. Dust off the tops of doors, windows and casings to make sure that there is no dust or dirt there.

If dust or dirt gets onto the paint while it is wet, you are better to let it dry and then sand down the surface and recoat. Be sure to remove the dust also before spraying.

Bleeding

What is it?

This is a common defect and is caused when something on the surface "bleeds" through the next coating. There are a number of causes for this, but the main cause is that the solvent in the paint re-activates a previous coating.

Typical examples of this are bitumen paint. This is reactivated by the white spirit of an oil based paint so that if it painted over the black comes through the new coating.

Another example is felt tip pen. This will reactivate when emulsion is painted over it.

Finally, a water stain on the ceiling or wall will "bleed" through and emulsion paint.

Solution

The solution is to seal the surface with a paint that has a different solvent to the coating which bleeds and therefore you will not activate it. The most commonly used sealer is Zinsser BIN. This is methylated spirit based and therefore will seal most coatings. It is also quick drying so that it does not hold the job up.

Water stains and felt tip pen can also be sealed with an oil based white undercoat (which you will usually already have) however this would take longer to dry before it could be recoated.

Blistering

What is it?

Generally caused by trapped moisture under the paint, either in the wood itself or between coats. When you scrape them off you will find that they are filled with water. The moisture expands in warm weather and causes the paint to blister.

Solution

Scrape off the blisters, allow to dry. Rub down and repaint. Make sure that you sand down the surface enough to remove the edge of the removed blister or alternatively you could use a fine filler to level the surface before re-painting.

Blooming

What is it?

A whitish appearance on the surface of the gloss, where the gloss has gone matt. Caused by moisture in the air when painting. This usually happens in the winter months if you gloss at the end of the day. There is really no heat in the sun and when dusk comes there is dampness in the air. This is absorbed into the drying paint causing it to lose its shine.

Solution

There is no point repainting unless the weather is warm and dry. I have done jobs where even if the gloss is applied mid-afternoon, it still blooms when it goes dark. To fix the problem the surface will need to be rubbed down and re-glossed on a warmer day.

Chalking

What is it?

Loss of gloss due to the erosion process of the paint film. This can apply to all paints however it usually is gloss paints that have weathered so that if you rub the surface with your hand the pigment comes off and the surface feels chalky.

Solution

Wash down the chalky paint with sugar soap and water. Rinse, sand down and the repaint with undercoat and gloss.

Cissing

What is it?

This is a common defect and is caused by paint being applied to a contaminated surface such as wax, grease, dirt or silicone. It can also happen if you paint water based paints on to surfaces previously painted with oil based paints. Cissing is where the paint fails for form a continuous film.

The best approach to avoid this problem is to wash the surface down with sugar soap which will remove any grease and dirt. Then rub down the surface to provide a key. This should be enough to prevent the defect.

Solution

If you do get the defect then you will need to allow the paint to dry, then flat down the surface wet or dry and repaint. Make sure that the surface is properly sanded as the previous coat which was cissing may not be properly adhered to the surface.

Curtaining (and runs)

What is it?

This one is very easy to produce with the airless sprayer. Because the paint is delivered so fast, any hesitation will cause too much paint to be applied to the surface and the paint will run and sag. These are called curtains, the good news is that you will quickly perfect your spraying technique so that this does not happen very often.

Solution

Try and resist the temptation to rectify the problem with a brush, although the problem looks like it can be brushed out you will find that the paint is very thick and attacking it with a with a brush will only make it worse. If the coating is emulsion then once it is dry rub down dry and the curtaining will rub out easily, you can then touch up as required.

If the paint is acrylic eggshell or gloss then wait for the coating to dry hard and then flat down using wet or dry sandpaper and then repaint.

Efflorescence

What is it?

This can be seen on new buildings usually and is a white salty deposit on the surface of the masonry, it is caused by moisture bringing out the salts in the walls. This cannot be painted over because the paint will not stick to the walls with the salty deposit there.

Solution

Scrape down and brush off the salts. Use contract emulsion as this allows the surface to breathe and the moisture to pass through the paint as it dries out.

Flaking

What is it?

This is a common defect on painted surfaces that have weathered over time, the paint film starts to break down and the paint flakes off. This defect however can appear more quickly if the surface is not prepared properly.

If the surface is not rubbed down with sandpaper to provide a "key" for the next layer of paint to stick to then you can get flaking. It can also be caused by contamination of the surface such as grease or polish.

If you suspect either of these on the surface then you will need to degrease with white spirit, methylated spirits or a degreaser.

Solution

Unfortunately, this is not an easy one to resolve because you will need to remove all the flaking paint, rub down and repaint.

Fingers or tails

What is it?

This is a spray defect where the paint does not atomise correctly, and you get lines on the wall. There are a number of causes of this.

The pressure may not be high enough, the paint may be too thick, the filter may be blocked causing the pressure to be lower at the tip and finally the sprayer may not be powerful enough to atomise the paint that you are using.

Solution

Turn the pressure up until you get a nice even spray pattern. It is very likely that this is the cause of the problem. If this does not work, then thin the paint until it atomises.

Change the filter if you think it may be blocked or try the next size up. Finally check the sprayer that you are using will work with the tip size and paint combination you have.

Flashing

What is it?

This problem can occur on any paint that has a sheen to it. It looks like a matt line or patches of uneven sheen in eggshell, silk or gloss.

This can be caused in two ways, firstly by the wet edge drying, for example if you were painting a wall in eggshell and you cut in around the edges first and then rolled the middle this could flash because the cutting in will be nearly dry by the time that you roll. It is less likely to happen with spraying because there is no cutting in and it is faster.

Secondly it can be caused by touching up. If a wall is marked and you touch the part up, then this will show.

Solution

You will need to rub down the area that is flashing and repaint the whole surface again up to a natural break such as a corner of a wall.

Grinning

What is it?

If you have a surface that is painted in a dark colour, for example dark blue and you are going to paint it white then it will take a few coats to cover. When you apply the first coat then the blue will grin through the white.

Some colours have poor "opacity" or covering power for example dark blues and reds. These will need additional coats to prevent grinning.

Solution

This is an easy one to solve as you will need to apply an additional coat to ensure coverage or maybe more additional coats depending on the colour change. It is worth bearing in mind that additional coats are easy with the sprayer as the main time is taken by masking. It is worth judging if the paint has covered before de masking.

Misses

What is it?

Misses are self-explanatory and amazingly quite common. Misses are patches where the paint has not been applied, either intentionally or not. These can be caused by poor light, careless painting or simply not painting something because it is not going to be seen.

Solution

If the coating is matt emulsion, then the solution is simple in that you can just touch up the missed areas. It is worth making sure that you have good light when you are painting, use site lamps to be sure that they can see what they are doing and minimising the problem. If the coating has a sheen then you will need to recoat and area up to an edge, for example the corner of a wall.

Mould

What is it?

Organic mould on an interior wall surface caused by damp conditions, it is a living thing and will grow and spread once that it has started to take hold.

Solution

Wash down with thinned bleach or fungicide solution. Make sure that you don't spread the problem by scraping it off dry and allowing the spores to spread. The area may need more than one treatment of the fungicide solution. Once the area is free from mould then you can repaint.

Orange peel

What is it?

This is not always a defect, it depends on your point of view. Orange peel can be produced both with a roller and a sprayer. It becomes a defect if the texture finish in the finished coating is not wanted.

If you roll emulsion onto a smooth plaster wall with a long pile roller, then you will get a heavy texture which is not wanted. If you are spraying paint which is too thick then you can get orange peel.

If you roll a wall with a medium pile roller, then you will get some orange peel, but this is usually acceptable.

Solution

This one is better to prevent before you start by either using the correct pile roller or making sure that you thin the paint to the correct consistency before spraying.

Using a short pile roller instead of a long pile roller when applying emulsion to a smooth surface.

Overspray

What is it?

Overspray is when paint goes where you do not want it to. Either by not masking correctly, for example a hinge may get paint on it because there is a gap in the masking or by paint carrying further then you anticipate getting paint on the surrounding area.

Solution

This has been discussed previously but it is worth noting that if you mask and sheet correctly and use a new tip and spray at the correct pressure then you will not get overspray.

If you do get paint on surfaces that you do not want it then it is worth cleaning it off straight away. Methylated spirit will clean off dry emulsion because it softens it. Warm water will work also on some surfaces.

Ropiness

What is it?

Ropiness is heavy brush marks in the paint (usually undercoat). When spraying these are already there and if not removed will show through your finish.

Solution

To prevent this when brushing you need to make sure that you thin the paint slightly if needed, use the correct brush for the paint you are using. Synthetic with acrylic undercoat. You can abrade the paint between coats to remove brush marks.

If I am spraying woodwork, then I use a power sander to remove the brush marks from the last redecoration. Once this is done you should not get them showing though on your final coat.

Saponification

What is it?

This is caused by Alkyd paint (like oil based gloss or eggshell) being in contact with Alkali (in plaster for example). The alkali reacts with the oils in the paint to prevent it drying and creates a sticky residue on the surface.

Solution

This is best prevented by not doing it in the first place and either using ARP (alkali resisting primer) or a water based system. If you do get the problem after the paint has been applied, then you will need to clean off the film with white spirit to remove the residue and then apply alkali resisting primer.

Yellowing

What is it?

This is the yellowing of oil based paints due to the oils used in the paint. It happens when there is a lack of light or a low level of light. It can commonly be seen on the backs of cupboard doors or under ornaments on the window cill.

This problem has got worse since the new VOC regulations have been introduced. Some white oil based glosses can yellow in a few weeks.

Solution

There are a couple of solutions to this problem. If the surface is re exposed to the light, then the yellowing will fade and the white surface will be restored. A better solution is to use none yellowing paints. These are basically acrylics.

Acrylic gloss is not a shiny as oil based gloss but they are not far off and they will not yellow. Acrylic paints are harder to apply by brush and get a decent finish however when applied by spray you will get a good finish with the added bonus of no yellowing.

Chapter 14 – The last one

I couldn't end the book talking about paint defects, it just doesn't seem right. I hope you have found this book useful. Different readers will get different things from this.

I have tried to keep the content easy to understand but also tried to cover all the bases. I had the following people in mind as I wrote.

Maybe you are a student and your teacher has given you this book as part of the course. In which case you may put it away and dig it out in five years' time muttering "Where did I put that book my teacher gave me, I am sure it was about spraying."

Maybe you are a decorator who is new to spraying. Yes, you did a bit at college, but you were not really paying attention. Now you have to bring home the bacon, spraying looks like a way to increase those all-important earnings.

Maybe you are a sprayer who has not done much lately, and it has inspired you to dust off your machine, get it serviced and get back out there producing some fast and flawless work with a new passion.

Maybe you are an experienced sprayer who just had to have that book on spraying that everyone was talking about.

Finally, you could be someone who has nothing to do with decorating at all and wants to find out what everyone is talking about when they say, "Airless spraying."

It is possible that you fall into a category that I have not thought of. Whatever your background I hope you take from this book that you too could get a little airless system for under a grand and start earning more money per day and start producing a finish that would rival any factory paint finish out there.

When I speak to customers, I never mention the speed, I focus on the "flawless" I spend the time that I save with the spraying on preparation so that the finish (especially woodwork) is remarkable. You can achieve a flawless finish by brush but believe me it's quicker and easier by spray.

When I speak to contractors (I work a lot for other decorators) I talk about the speed. This is the "fast" in Fast and Flawless. Many do not believe the quoted times until they see it for themselves. I love to spray a door in front of an experienced decorator and watch them start doing the maths in their head.

I have spent many training days with decorators, showing them how to use the equipment and try and banish some of the common myths that surround spraying. It only usually takes a day and they are flying on their own. I speak to them days or weeks later and they start quoting times at me.

"I priced the job for fourteen days and I did it in four, I just have a permanent smile on my face" one happy decorator reported back.

Another said to me as we worked "I have just mist coated that room in 6 minutes, unbelievable."

Whilst spaying a three-story apartment building the comment was, "It's only took us three days, this is a £2,500 job!"

Whilst spraying a rough render outside the apprentice said "It's only took forty five minutes to put one coat on, I think we will be finished for dinner. That's good I could do to go up town this afternoon and buy some clothes for my holiday" That made me smile, we were all young once eh?

Once decorators start saying these things to me, I know that they have joined the exclusive club of Fast and Flawless sprayers.

Hopefully one day you will join us.

About the author

Pete Wilkinson has been decorating all of his life. He currently teaches Painting and decorating part time and also runs Pete Wilkinson Decorators. He lives in Preston with his partner Tracey and in the very rare time off likes to relax on his boat.

If you want to get more involved, we run spraying courses in Preston (North West), Edenbridge (South East), Exeter (South West), Glenrothes (Scotland) and Ireland.

Check out our website; -

www.painttechtrainingacademy.co.uk

Once you have completed the course, we offer ongoing support as you start spraying on your own jobs. You will gain entry to a private members forum called "PTA support".

Only people who have done the course are in this forum and the idea is to offer ongoing advice and support.

Finally, we run a Facebook forum called "Spraying Makes Sense" it's free to join and you will get lots of hints and tips on spraying from people who are experienced in the trade.

Other books by the author

Fast and Flawless Pricing – A guide to pricing and business for decorators

Are you a decorator that struggles with pricing? Have you just set up in business and are looking for some pointers?

Are you an established business looking for some inspiration on how to move forward? This chatty guide on pricing and business will gently guide you through the process of pricing a decorating job. It looks at the pitfalls of getting your pricing wrong and the advantages of having a good pricing system.

The book has been written by someone who has both been a decorator and taught decorating in a local college for most of his life.

Fast and Flawless Systems – A Decorators guide to planning and carrying out successful job

This book looks at systems for Decorators.

This book covers all types of systems from which paint to use on what surface to what order you should spray a room. The book also covers aspects of decorating that you may or may not be aware of such as painting uPvc, training, funding and marketing.

If you have read the other two books already then this is one is a must read, if you haven't then this book is a great place to start.

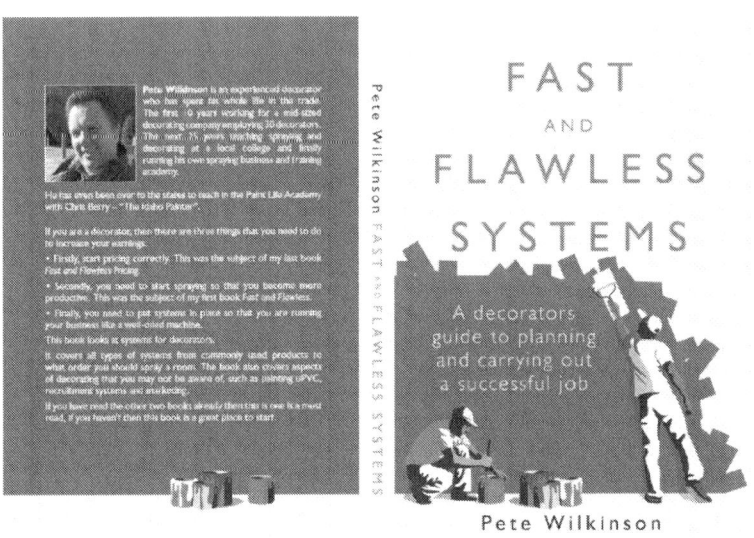

Tales from the building site - Lessons learned when working on a big site

The author has spent many years working in the building trade as a decorator. During all those years he has seen things that have made him laugh and things that have made him tear his hair out.

There have also been many occasions that have made him proud to be part of it all. Here is a book for all you people in the trade and also for everyone else who wonders what goes on behind those big high hoardings that clearly state the public are not allowed in.

It is a warts and all look behind the curtain from the perspective of a decorator. Be prepared to be shocked, to laugh and to shake your head in disbelief.

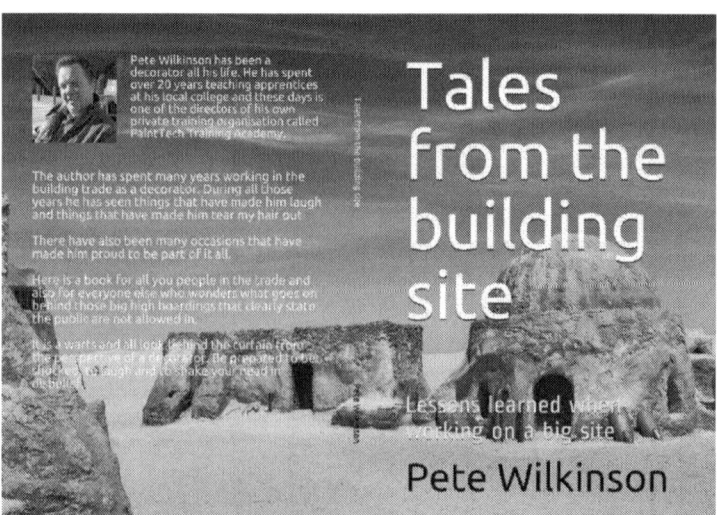

Boat Life – The trials and tribulations of living aboard a boat

Nothing to do with construction or decorating. I love boats, I have one and I have lived aboard myself, so this is an insight into the lifestyle.

This is a book for boaters, written by a boater. Pete Wilkinson has spent his whole life around boats and has owned a couple too.

The book looks at all aspects of boating including, what is the best boat to buy, where to look when buying a boat and do you build one or do you buy one?

The following questions are answered; - Which is the best type of boat - Wood fibreglass or steel? Do you borrow money or save to get your boat? Do you move around or stay put? What is the essential kit needed? How do you keep her shipshape?

The book also looks at living board and gives an insight into the liveaboard life. The book also puts boating into the context of modern life and discusses the advantages of living on board.

Finally, if you have wondered what goes on behind the curtain of a boater's life then this book will show you.

Check out the website

If you are interested in being kept up to date with future books or you just fancy the odd freebee then subscribe on my website.

www.fastandflawless.co.uk

Glossary of terms

Airless sprayer

This is a type of spray equipment that uses a high pressure pump to spray paint. The paint is at 2000 psi when it comes out of the tip and this is enough to atomise it without the use of air.

Atomise

This is when paint is broken into a fine mist and can therefore be sprayed.

Bounce back

If you spray either too close to the surface or at too high a pressure then the paint can bounce back from the surface causing a type of overspray.

Cleanshot valve

A device made by Graco which fits on the end of your extension pole to prevent spitting. This is an extra valve in the end of the pole which shuts off the flow of paint when you release the trigger at the gun.

Diaphragm pump

A pump design, different from the piston pump (some would say better) which uses a flexible membrane and pulsating hydraulic fluid to produce pressure. Check out the Wagner Finish range.

Electronic pressure control

This regulates the pressure electronically rather than mechanically to provide a more precise control.

Fan size

The spray fan is the width of the spray pattern on the wall when the gun is 12" from the wall. This is shown by the first number on the tip. For example, 517 would give a 10" fan pattern. (Multiply the first number by two).

Fine finish tip

This is a specially designed tip for better atomisation for use on surfaces where a better finish is needed such as doors and skirting. Wagner make a Fine Finish tip. Tritech make an Ultrafinish tip.

GPM

Gallons per minute.

Inlet ball

The ball part of the inlet valve of the fluid section of the airless sprayer. This acts as a check valve when sucking in paint. This can sometimes stick when the sprayer has been in storage.

Inlet tube

This is the large tube that is put into the paint or material to be sprayed.

Orifice

The hole in the tip that the paint passes through. This is a very small hole and is measured in thousandths of an inch. This is shown by the second part of the number stamped on the tip. For example 517 is a 17 thousandths of an inch orifice. The size of the hole controls the amount of paint that is put on the surface. The bigger the hole the more paint is put on.

Overspray

This is where the paint in the form of a mist goes beyond the surface you are spraying and settles on something you don't want it too. Easily avoided by good technique and masking.

Packings

The material used to make the piston liquid tight and therefore build pressure. These need changing every couple of years.

Pole

AKA extension pole, this screws on the end of your gun to give you more reach. Available in several sizes. These can be used to paint ceilings or to make spraying walls easier. These can be screwed together to give extra reach if needed.

Pressure roller

This is a roller that fits on the end of an extension pole and is fed paint by the airless sprayer. This eliminates the need to keep dipping the roller in paint and in theory creates less overspray.

Priming

This is where you charge the pump with paint and remove air from the system so that the pressure can be built up. Usually done when setting up but may need to be done if you run out of paint while spraying and draw in air.

Pump armour

A liquid that is put into the pump that protects it from frost and rust while in storage. Similar to antifreeze in a car engine.

Return tube

The smaller tube that returns the material back into the paint container when the pump is in prime mode.

Spray fan

The pattern that the sprayer makes when spraying. Usually a sharp line. This will soften to an oval when worn.

Spray tip

This slots into the tip guard and is the business end of the airless sprayer. This controls the fan width and the amount of paint sprayed onto the surface. These wear and need to be changed when done.

Throat seal liquid

AKA "TSL" This is a lubricant that is placed in a small cup at the top of the piston to keep the packings wet and lubricated. This needs to be done every four hours of continuous use.

Viscosity

This is how thick or thin the paint is and is measured with a viscosity cup which allows you to time the speed that paint flows. The faster it flows the thinner it is.

Whip hose.

> A thinner flexible piece of hose between the end of the high pressure hose and the gun. This is more flexible and makes for an easier day spraying.

Printed in Great Britain
by Amazon